"Quick, knowledgeable, colorful and irreverent— a talented and very smart man."

—New York Times

GARY McCORD

still plays in several tournaments a year, and is partner with Peter Kostis in the Kostis/McCord Learning Center in Scottsdale, Arizona. He is a playing editor for *Golf Digest*, writes regularly for America Online's iGolf service, appeared as himself and was technical golf director for the movie *Tin Cup*, and wrote (with John Huggan) *Golf for Dummies*. He lives in Scottsdale, Arizona, and Avon, Colorado.

ALSO BY GARY McCORD

Golf for Dummies (with John Huggan)

Just a Range Ball in a Box of Titleists®

On and Off the Tour
with Gary McCord

Berkley Books
NEW YORK

JUST A RANGE BALL IN A BOX OF TITLEISTS®

A Berkley Book / published by arrangement with
the author

PRINTING HISTORY
G. P. Putnam's Sons edition / March 1997
Published simultaneously in Canada
Berkley trade paperback edition / April 1998

Book design by Laura Hammond Hough.

The Penguin Putnam Inc. World Wide Web site address is
http://www.penguinputnam.com

ISBN: 0-425-16164-1

BERKLEY®
Berkley Books are published by
The Berkley Publishing Group, a division of Penguin Putnam Inc.,
375 Hudson Street, New York, New York 10014.
BERKLEY and the "B" design are trademarks
belonging to Penguin Putnam Inc.

PRINTED IN THE UNITED STATES OF AMERICA

10 9 8 7 6

To

My granddaughters, Breanne, Kayla, Genae, and Terra. These words will help a little toward your sojourn through college. To my sister, Karen, and my parents, I really did write this! To Alan "Mad Dog" Skuba, I apologize for the long hours of editing, but you've got nothing to do anyway. And finally, to my wife, Diane, my life's psychagogue. Steer me clear.

P.S.

To all the boys and girls at San Luis Rey Downs, thanks for being a lesion on society.

Contents

Introduction

I fought this for a long time. This book-writing thing. Hours and hours of flailing away at my computer with no compass to guide me. I don't want to be indoors. My life has been a pursuit of that stupid little white orb that won't go into the hole quick enough. Golf is a mindless game played by the quick-witted. I am mindless and yearn to be outdoors, so leave me alone to be absorbed by the environment.

The first book, *Golf for Dummies*, took much of my daylight for the latter part of '95. I had to sit in an uncomfortable chair for days on end and rot in front of a thirteen-inch video monitor. My retinas cried for real light. I got cranky and became sterile during this time. The book was completed on deadline and I was a hero to my publisher. That's something I will take to my grave, where I'll be bedded down with eternal peace licking at my soul.

But what's this! My agent informs me that another book is a must while your journalistic journey is ripe. We had a publisher ready to go (Putnam) and I could write anything I wished. I was writing the last book while on the set of the movie *Tin Cup*, and that proved very difficult. I told my agent, "Hell no!"

Like most agents, he doesn't listen well.

I'm glad I penned these essays. The mere fact I wrote every word of this epistle has a satisfaction and fulfillment in this period of ghostwriters and tape-recorded interpretations. I wish all my brethren in the sports world would take the time and write their work, without persiflage of an author-for-hire, and the buying public could really see how screwed up most of us really are. This writing is a great stew for the soul.

I've had a rare glimpse of life afforded me through golf. I have urinated in public with Fairway Louie and played golf with presidents. I have been welcomed at my course, San Luis Rey Downs, and kicked out of Augusta National. I grew up with guys named Steve "Mad Max" Huffman and Willie "Brain Damage" Rains and now go to clubs that have "Chad and Buffy" on the membership roster. I've met some of the nicest people on the planet doing a Hollywood movie, *Tin Cup*, and have been bored to death at most charitable social functions. Life's merry-go-round is golf, grab the ring.

These essays have touched every facet of my experience. If you have a preconceived idea that I'm a little left of the plumb bob, that interpretation will be enhanced after you peruse this book. Hopefully, you will enjoy this nonsense as much as I have enjoyed writing it.

It was best said by my mentor, as we sat on the deck of the caboose at San Luis Rey Downs during a controlled beer experiment: "I am never alone, I have my passion. I sit in the chamber of this contradiction. I'm having a bowel movement, and it is golf."

Fairway Louie, circa 1982.

McCordisms: A Glossary

1. THE CELLOPHANE BRIDGE—a putt that crawls over the lip
2. A RUPAUL—a double cross. To aim for a slice and hit a hook, or vice versa
3. FOUNTAIN BALL—a drive that goes too high
4. SPANK THOSE WHITE BOYS—to hit range balls
5. FULL FLAPS—a ball that is rolling or flying too far
6. JAMES BOND STROKE—a putting stroke that is shaken, not stirred
7. BALATA FLUSH—a putt that goes in
8. THE SAMSONITE SLIDE—a golfer who plays badly on Saturday at a PGA Tour event
9. WORM CAM—a camera view on the ground
10. PULL A HAMSTRING—a putt that needs to slow down
11. SKID ROW—a low, unfortunate shot
12. A ROSEANNE—a shot that is hit fat
13. A VIN SCULLY—a skulled shot
14. THE BEN WRIGHT RANGE—a putt you cannot miss
15. LIKE STRIKING OUT THE PITCHER—a putt you cannot miss
16. A SHRIMP—a duck-hook
17. NUKE IT—hit the hell out of it

18. YASIR ARAFAT—ugly and in the sand
19. MORGAN FAIRCHILD—a good-looking shot, but a little thin
20. GROW HAIR, BALL—requesting a putt to slow down
21. BODY BAGS, TAG ON HIS TOE, CALL THE CORONER—a ball that is dead
22. LONG-EARED SOCIETY—Masters committee
23. BENNY HANNA—a chop
24. MICHAEL JACKSON'S "MOONWALK"—a ball that backs up on the green
25. FIRE UP THE ZAMBONI MACHINE—greens are getting fast
26. EDWARD SCISSORHANDS ROUGH—rough so deep, he couldn't get it out
27. WORSE THAN GRANDMA'S UNDERWEAR—an ugly shot
28. DO THE HEIMLICH ON HIM—he's choking
29. THEY'VE BIKINI-WAXED 'EM—what I got kicked out of the Masters telecast for saying (fast greens)
30. BAT TURN—a putt that lips out
31. GEORGE JEFFERSON—"moving on up" the leader board
32. PICTURE ON THE MILK CARTONS—playing so badly nobody has seen you lately
33. BOB MARLEY—he smoked a "big one" by you
34. MICK JAGGER—a lip-out
35. PEARL JAM—ramming in a short putt
36. ROADKILL—a ball hit into the gallery
37. CALL THE PSYCHIC FRIENDS HOTLINE—a putt you cannot read
38. BILINGUAL ILLITERATE—can't read the putt from either direction

39. SHIRLEY MACLAINE—a putt that can go many directions
40. YOU CAN HEAR YOUR OWN LUNG COLLAPSE—very quiet on the golf course
41. I'M SUCKING LIKE A CHEST WOUND—having a bad day on the course
42. HE'S GOT TO CHANGE HIS UNDERWEAR—a remarkable shot
43. HE NEEDS A PUTTER ENEMA—your putter needs a bowel movement
44. SMOKING GROOVES—lots of back-suck on a ball hitting the green
45. GRASS SLOTH—a slow player
46. NOT MUCH DIFFERENCE BETWEEN A RUT AND A GROOVE—fine line between playing good and bad
47. RUN LIKE YOU STOLE SOMETHING—requesting a golf ball to get going
48. BEAT IT LIKE A RENTED MULE—hit the hell out of it
49. GOLF—an itch you can't scratch
50. WILY SCAVENGER—a cunning golfer who gets it up and down at will
51. THAT'S GOT SOME ENTERTAINMENT VALUE—a well-executed shot that draws a golf clap from the gallery
52. GRASS COFFIN—where your golf ball lies is dead
53. IF UGLY IS A HAMBURGER, THAT'S A WHOPPER—a real ugly shot
54. KING MISSILE AND THE FREE ATMOSPHERE—a flier out of the rough
55. DARTH FADER—a slice
56. CHARLES BARKLEY—a ball that hits a tree
57. WEIRD AL YANKOVIC—a pulled tee shot

58. JOAN RIVERS, RICKI LAKE, CHARLIE WATERS—a ball in the agua
59. DONNER PARTY—this shot will eat you alive
60. MOSS GROWING ON YOUR NORTH SIDE—dark, wet conditions
61. ADRIFT ON THE SARTORIAL SEAS—bad golf outfit
62. WOODEN MIND AND A STEEL ATTITUDE—thick-headed individual
63. HORMEL—a chili dip, a shot with more turf than ball

The Boneyard

The Boneyard

There exists a place for the golfer that is a sanctuary for his soul to contemplate the very existence of his being. It defines his social status as a golfer and his spiritual worth. It is the very belly of the devil, and the halo of the deity, all in one. If you choose this path of professional golf you have asked yourself many questions as to your existence in this furnace of ambivalence. We call it: The Rock Pile, Study Hall, The Launching Pad, The Blister Box, The Range, The Boneyard. It is the place of friendly advice.

For as long as I can remember, there has been a "range" involved in my daily lifestyle. This is where I got my schooling on the nature of flight. It is where I learned my vocation, not to mention sex, drugs, and rock 'n' roll. It was a study hall for life, and I visited it daily. My first conscious thought as a person was when I hung out at Riverside Golf Range. My age was thirteen, and I was in the depths of a testosterone body flush.

Golf was for geeks in those days, so I continued to play baseball and basketball so I could have some kind of social status. But The Range provided a field of fascination that, to this day, let me explore with the teenage zest of my puberty years. I am a grass pilot.

I remember the first time The Range really scared me. I was

preparing for the toughest medieval exercise of a golfer's life: the Qualifying School; a place Hitler must have used to develop his keen sense of worth. The year was 1973. Three hundred seventy players entered the "Q" school, and twenty-three of us got our cards. The lottery has better odds.

I prepared four months in advance for the school by hitting one thousand balls a day. To this day, I do not know what I was working on, but somebody, probably an elder, monastic, lost soul of the soil, encouraged me to hit one thousand balls a day if I ever was going to "make it." I remember that dark hole of perdition as I counted to one thousand armed only with my clubs, lunch, and some Band-Aids. I learned the greatest lesson of my golfing life there in that hole. Discipline. The very act of getting up on my own and trudging down to The Range and hitting balls from eight in the morning till dusk with only fifteen minutes reserved for lunch, when I should have been out chasing girls, proved to me I was nuts at an early age. What mystical force drove me? Was I some sort of Taoist monk who had just read *Zen and the Birds of Appetite*, concerned with the order of the universe? Had something spiritually jumped into my leptosome body and flushed me with context?

No, I believe I was motivated to succeed. I wanted something and went out to get it. Discipline got in the way of youth.

I received my card that year and went on to doom and obscurity on the PGA Tour. But what an "E" ticket ride it was. The Range was where the gladiators gathered. It was our social bosom. The place where we developed our personalities or shunned them completely. It is the place where we got all of our free stuff. The equipment manufacturers circled us like polyester buzzards giving us golf merchandise we could either collect or give away next Christmas. It's a great place.

The Range is a free social area from Monday through Wednesday. People of all denominations roam free and listen to their favorite pro speak of the incantations of the game. They can listen to all of the sport psychologists wave their magical spells over the afflicted, wounded golfer. They can hear gurus teach the fine art of movement in time and space with reference to the flight of the ball. Obi Wan Kenobi would have been a hit on The Range.

You can hear the caddies, our beasts of burden, talk the talk and get a wager on their man against yours for a sporting fee. They are all optimistic early in the year. The social status of the Tour is defined here. No other place is worthy.

Starting on Thursday, the atmosphere on The Range becomes dense. The problems of the day are to be addressed. It is the first day of the tournament. We do not know what is to unfold. I warm up and feel optimistic. That doesn't last long. A certain position feels a little awkward, so I change the trajectory of an arm. Whoops! Now my right leg is locking. Must point left foot more clockwise at address. Now the left eye is starting to blur. What is happening? Pretty soon my caddie is going up and down the driving range trying to buy out of all his bets. Golf brain has entered my realm. I'm doomed to shoot 78. Are there enough sport psychologists and gurus to go around? I need clinical help!

After the round is over, there exists on The Range a feudal state. There are princes and paupers. The guys who have played well are out there chirping, telling everybody in earshot how good they played the par-3s. They are loose and full of answers. Not too loud, for tomorrow may bring, as Leonard Pinth Garnell says, "Bad Golf." Today's answers may bring tomorrow's questions. The longer you play the Tour, the more you realize that.

The guys who played the day without distinction usually have a certain vague look in their eyes. Kind of like the eyes of an armadillo in your headlights just before becoming road kill. Glazed, but aware. These guys have golf clubs lying everywhere on the ground for alignment problems. They're hitting balls twice as fast as the guys who have played well. They are not looking around to see who is watching. Their caddies are attentive and have that broken look about them. They are both seeking answers, but do not know the question.

It is The Range, and all of the golfing world resides here. Spank those white boys, they tell the truth. Patois of the insane.

The Smell of Golf

The wafting smell of golf is one that is neglected or forgotten until that time when something so pungent shakes your golf brain. It's a jukebox of smells, some so powerful they recall your crib when you were a child and that sweet smell of baby vomit as you reflected on nursing a four-footer down the hill to win the Open. I must have been nursing on the wrong thing.

The recollection of smells that permeated my brain when golf was a new toy still commands strong feelings of puberty and the rites of discovery. Those long days when my parents would deliver me to the baby-sitter, Muni. Off I went, bag hoisted over my shoulder to walk the fairways until my parents signaled their return to the parking lot with a cadence of flashing lights. I was in love with this alluring creature, Golf. I had no idea of the technique, but was long on stamina.

The smell of fresh-cut grass is the almighty aphrodisiac that golfers recall. If you have evolved with this game from the onset of wonder, you have enriched your brain with the smell of freshly cut grass. Bent, rye, Bermuda, poa annua, whatever the derivation, the smell is there forever for you to revisit.

The world was slower then, and the golf swing was longer.

Flexibility and energy were the components that made this game all-consuming, and a keen sense of smell brings back those long summer days in the aroma of the grass.

Those tender days of annoying aromas were forever attached to my brain with the recollection of smells from my favorite golf pro, Gordon Macintosh. He came to this country with a big hook and a bigger drinking problem. Gordon presided over one of Riverside's favorite municipal golf courses. It is no longer there; it is now a Kmart Future City site. I will miss the madness.

The Muni was a petri dish of smells. The summer days were filled with smog and sweat. The dingy clubhouse was musty and dank. The old head pro was awash in scotch. When he passed, it was enough to make a young man drunk. Plaids were prevalent as Gordon redeemed his past.

Gordon had a parrot named George that was ever present on his shoulder. The bird smelled of tired feathers and was nicknamed Hawkeye. He was given the name because Gordon no longer had full use of his sight, and it was the parrot's job to warn unsuspecting golfers to beware of one of Gordon's wayward shots. If Gordon let go with one of his characteristic hooks, the pugnacious parrot was taught to say "watch out" in a high, shrill voice. He monitored Gordon's every step, and "watch out" became a musical accompaniment to Gordon's shuffling feet. I hear the parrot finally died of emphysema.

Not only did the pro and the parrot maintain the pro shop, they supervised the snack shop and all the foul-smelling food that made the health inspector cringe. Road kill left in the wake of a Peterbilt on a hot summer's day smelled better. If you opened the door to the snack shop and the wind was determined, the pro shop took on the flavor of a Coney Island hot dog stand that was cooking mystery meat hot dogs.

Those smells curbed my appetite forever. The olfactory response to my adolescence on the golf course is a firestorm of memories. The turgid stench of the water in the pre-colonial range-ball-washing apparatus that I slaved over nightly could not be unlike the smell a dog must encounter as he drinks from the commode.

My wild youth and the exhaust from the ancient golf carts collided every morning as I armed them for their day's emissions. The cart barn was dark and underground. It was made in the days of preventilation. The exhaust could not escape and my lungs and nose were the home for the contaminants. My nose hairs are permanently scorched and that smell reminds me of $1.50 an hour.

As I would exit the cavern of combustion around 8 A.M., the shifting wind in the summer would stray the stench of the retro-rot in the scum-filled lake surrounding the ninth green toward the clubhouse. That smell, combined with the coffee that was being brewed by the pro and the parrot in their snack shop from hell, is responsible for the decline of the West.

My odoriferous mind will never forget these lifelong odors of a well-spent youth. The only aroma I never experienced was the sweet smell of success on the Tour. Must have been the mutilated nose hairs.

"Keep your head to the path and your nose to the wind."

The Downs

Big Divorces and Small Divots

I have paraded around this golfing world with a ticket to divine sanctuary, my PGA Tour card. It has accessed me to venues of exquisite beauty. Towering palm trees of the Hawaiian Islands, the emerald green landscape of Ireland, the rugged terrain and noble beauty of Australia. All have eclipsed my brow as I have been searching the fairways of life.

The sheer grandeur and pageantry of this game has nestled within my soul. It levels the spirit and hides the anticipation of death. Golf is life's motivational speech.

As I glance back, beyond the alamedas of the world's greatest golf courses, I discover a place of awakening. The womb of enlightenment. The place in which all of life's dark treaties were negotiated to simple thought and careless action. That place where refuge and lifelong association are housed.

Your persona has been formed by social, environmental, and spiritual awakenings. You don't cast those manuscripts of life upon the wind and let them settle into some corner of this cockeyed world. You form those social skills early. Man is socially mutable, and I came from the land of the idiots.

I have no recollection of abuse from my childhood. I was a

good child from good parents. I did as they told me and stayed away from trouble in the difficult time of the sixties. Sports was my social catalyst. I was antiseptically clean and nurtured in a sterile corral.

As I started the Tour in 1974 and moved from Riverside, California, to Escondido, California, past and present collided. I came from Victoria Country Club in Riverside, a posh club that had roots back to 1908. The membership was as old as the furniture. I learned much about my golf game there, but socially I was a runt. Then came San Luis Rey Downs Golf and Country Club, a public facility that could have been called an asylum.

Order had now changed to disorder. In the long run of things, here is how it will be played out. Solar energy, the product of a hot sun turning in cold space, will eventually burn out. Molecular chaos will prevail, and we'll all be left sitting in a lukewarm cosmic bath watching our dicks fall off. Except at San Luis Rey, where Fairway Louie will be asking our bookie, Unemployed Lloyd, what's the price on the game this week and can he play on house money until he sells his double-wide to pay off last week's losses? San Luis Rey is such a mutation that cataclysmic events will not persuade the place to die. Charles Darwin never met Fairway Louie and the boys.

I was introduced to "Head Pro" in January of 1974. There had been an awful fire that had destroyed the pro shop and all of the saleable inventory. What a shame, all that spectacular stuff the public hadn't bought for the last three and a half years was now dark polyester fire remnants. Luckily, the fire insurance had been paid, the week prior.

Head Pro told me of the time-consuming efforts that were now in place to "remodel" the old shop so it would look like new. They had already brought in the double-wide mobile home and had anchored it and placed potted daisies around the periphery to appease the women's twilight league.

The golf course, twenty-six-room lodge, and thoroughbred racing facility had been recently sold to Millie Vessels, who had just lost her husband, Frank, to an unfortunate shooting death. Millie Vessels came into town in her white Lincoln Continental limousine, with a wad of insurance money, a fondness for drink, and questions about her husband's death.

The golf course is a pretty good layout. There is a nursery of grasses in the fairways, poa-annua greens that you need help from the Psychic Friends Network to read, plus various dead trees that the native wildlife (illegal aliens) burn to keep warm at night. The golf course wanders around a floodplain that is constantly moist from California floods. The stream carries the overflow and is always harassing the fairways. Mud golf is always fun in the winter. Encroaching never lessens the fun at the "Downs" because there is always a wager in the air. Silt or no silt.

I grew so fond of this place that I became a resident of the place after my divorce. I had little left in the way of real property after my marriage. A 1974 Mercedes-Benz, some old Munsingwear golf shirts, a table clock given to me by an uncle who is doing time for forgery, and three sets of golf clubs. Just enough to start a new life amongst the derelicts. There was an old train caboose the club had fixed up and put on the golf course as a snack shop. It was six hundred square feet and had a nice porch on which I could entertain my guests. There was a john adjacent to the caboose and plenty of green grass. I moved in, and like my life, I was bringing up the rear in my new abode.

The cast of characters that made up this denizen of derelicts were my friends. They made fun of my bad play on the Tour and defended my right to exist when I was home. They were my cradle of insanity.

There was my junior college and college mentor, Fairway Louie. He taught me more about life than Phil Donahue. We had two bookies at the Downs; one was Willie "Brain Damage" Rains, who had a tattoo on each cheek of his ass with the letter "W" inscribed. When he mooned you, it spelled "WOW." Think about it. He was clever, too; sometimes he would moon you upside down and it would spell "MOM." Willie wasn't the best of bookies, but he was honest. A tribute rare among that species.

Our other bookie was Unemployed Lloyd, who never had a job, but always had his beeper on. Unemployed and Brain Damage were always fighting over spreads and neither had any money. A tribute rare among that species.

There was The Kitchen. He was the size of a Hugo and cost more to run. He had a three handicap, but on the kitchen table he was tour material. I saw him eat forty-three Twinkies at one sitting on a bet with some local gamesters. The Kitchen weighed 428 pounds, all fat.

There were two Vietnam veterans: Mad Max and Lock & Load. Mad Max, for fun, delivered pizzas in Cambodia during his tenure in Vietnam. He was a great wheelman and existed on one and a half hours of sleep. No matter how early you got to the Downs, Mad Max was there before you, staring at his coffee, complaining about his insurance business.

Lock & Load still has a passion for guns. He subscribes to those survivalist magazines and has more guns than a Third World country. He had me over to his "arsenal," to what he called his home, and showed me the new grenade launcher he had just bought. The guy has some wiring missing. He was always neatly attired in his camouflage fatigues and his Hawaiian golf shirt. He had some combat boots fitted with spikes. He wasn't meant to play golf.

The two horse trainers who frequented the golf course from the adjoining racetrack facilities were Muzzy and Packy. They were trainers for the thoroughbred horses of the rich and famous and they loved to play golf. They got into more trouble than Dennis Rodman trying to put on his wedding dress.

Always in the lounge was 20/20. He was legally blind, but loved to play gin and drive golf carts. 20/20 was supposedly blinded by a Gypsy curse, although we could never verify it.

You could also find The Breathalyzer. He had so many DWIs he wasn't allowed to drive. As the judge said, "Until Satan drives you to Hell." He had so many Breathalyzer tests he had "Listerine" embroidered on his golf bag as his official sponsor.

On the golf course you could find Master Sergeant Fenemore "Roots" Washington. He served at nearby Camp Pendleton for twenty-three years and then took over the green superintendent's job at the base's golf course. He retired when most of the base was shut down and came to work at San Luis Rey. He was a strict disciplinarian and could grow grass on aluminum. Roots was in charge of fifteen illegal aliens who worked on the golf course. His biggest concern was keeping the INS out of the maintenance barn and losing his workers to their homeland, Mexico.

The foreman of this maintenance crew was a Honduran National we named Chez-Juan. He was a slight man of dubious gender. Chez-Juan would arrive at work wearing glorious white Purcell sneakers and short socks equally as white. He would have on freshly pressed Byblos walking shorts that were cuffed. On his torso would be a Jockey tank top that was aflame with pastel colors. His neck would be highlighted by a gleaming scarf and his head would be bare except for black curly hair that was always maintained with a razor cut. He had some medallions hanging vaguely down his cleavage and a tattoo on his right forearm that said, "Vamanos." He was a darling. He also could operate every bit of machinery that Roots had with care and precision.

The indoor people were equally as divergently adrift. The starter in the double-wide was a bald hairdresser named Colonel Klink. The head professional was an unassuming former muffler installer at Sears Automotive who had taken the job on two different occasions. The manager of the club, Joe, worked at night managing the local topless bar.

The bartender, Paul, or as we call him, Quick Pour, had his two ex-wives working for him as waitresses. It's a festive night in the lounge where all have gathered and Quick Pour is screwing up drink orders. The two ex's are reminding him of his past failures, but we can't hear the interaction because the country-and-western band, Los Gringos, is over the legal decibel limit. All is well on this Friday night at the Downs.

It would be very difficult to pick just one circumstance that has caught my attention during the twenty-three years I have been hanging around the Downs. They all blend into chaos. I do remember one particular Friday that should have warranted a guest appearance on *Geraldo*.

It was a beautiful July morning during the summer of '83. The early-morning fog had just ascended and the smell of freshly mown grass was biting the air. It was Friday. Friday the thirteenth. This was a special day at San Luis Rey Downs. It was the day of the tournament we called the "Ex-Wives Conflict." We got the idea when

Quick Pour hired his two ex-wives to work in his bar. The format was simple—you played golf with your ex-wife in a nine-hole worst-ball tournament. You both teed off and played the worst shot until the ball had been holed. It was the format from hell, but our spouses had put us through worse. There were sixteen people signed up to play. Four foursomes of dysfunctional relationships trying to act civil in a hostile environment. I love this game.

I had arrived early at the golf course to meet Fairway Louie and the rest of the guys. It was 6:15 and we were to join Packy and Muzzy at the thoroughbred training facility. It was the day the horses were going swimming. There was a large pool in which injured thoroughbreds would swim and rehabilitate their injuries. It was also the chance to bet on who would win the thoroughbred freestyle. Packy and Muzzy would release the big ponies and we would be at the other end of the pool wildly exhorting our chosen thoroughbred to victory. This is not normal behavior.

We all wandered over to the dining room at the golf course for our daily consumption of lukewarm animal fat and powdered eggs. The talk at the table was centered around Packy and Muzzy's Colorado deer-hunting trip from which they had recently returned. The boys didn't have much luck with their hunting, but they were all equipped for the parade through the deer check at Wolcott, Colorado. As they were coming down the mountain on the last day of hunting season, there was a long line of off-road vehicles with various carcasses strapped to their fronts. Fish and Game officers were combing the vehicles as they approached the checkpoint and making sure the hunters had not bagged more than the legal limit.

As Packy and Muzzy approached, there was a look of astonishment on the faces of the Fish and Game boys. Muzzy was "buck" naked lying on the hood of the rented Jeep Grand Cherokee. He was roped on with his head hanging over the front end of the Jeep. There was blood poured all over his body. Driving the car was Packy, with a full deer's outfit on, complete with hooves. The deer, Packy, stopped the car and wanted to know where a good taxidermist was for his prize human. The officers waved them through and immediately closed the checkpoint.

There were fourteen of us at our regular breakfast table next to the window overlooking the toxic creek. Beatrice was our waitress. She was a grandmotherly woman of generous weight. She moved faster than she should be able to, but our food was never served on time. Beatrice had a hard life. She'd migrated from Des Moines, Iowa, where her farm had been foreclosed and then her husband hanged himself in the barn with her apron. Beatrice never wore an apron again. She remarried a substitute teacher and moved next to the seventh fairway in a leased condo. Their life sucked, but she was our favorite waitress. We tipped her accordingly.

The owner had just arrived, Millie Vessels. She sat in her customary place in the corner where she could watch what went on. It must be 9:30 A.M. She was prompt to a fault. We heard from Beatrice that there was another terrible fight between Millie and her son, Scoop, last night at dinner. Scoop ran the Downs, but is ever in conflict with his mother.

"What kind of fight this time?" asked Mad Max. He was on his seventh cup of coffee since awaking at 3:15 this beautiful morning.

"After they got their entrée, both had the special, rack of

Spam au jus. They started this terrible fight about who invented Spam. Millie was in a paroxysm of rage. She claimed a guy named Roy invented Spam. Scoop disagreed. She flung her mashed potatoes at him with an over-the-top motion and hit Scoop in the chest. He retaliated with a slice of Spam, hitting her in the middle of her beehive hairdo. It stuck. Words and food were flying. She stormed out of the dining room, but not before she fired everyone in the restaurant, including Scoop."

"How come you're still working this morning?" asked Fairway Louie.

"She did the same thing last week, but forgot about it the next day." Scoop walked in and sat down with his mother. They exchanged high fives.

Head Pro came in and asked what the pairings should be for the day. This was a delicate matter. Most of these adversarial marriages had ended in a serenade of slander. The ex-wives actually looked forward to each Friday the thirteenth as an excuse to inflict more mental duress on my buddies. The boys, on the other hand, thought maybe they could get a romp in the rack from their ex's. The plots gained in complexity.

We decided Mad Max's ex-wife, Tanya, should not be in the same group as The Breathalyzer's ex-wife, Noreen, because they were dating the same guy, Miguel. He was a waiter at the Sizzler in Bonsall. The Kitchen was bringing his ex-wife, Linda, who most of us could use as a shade tree. She tipped the scales at just under 350 pounds. We couldn't put both of them in the same golf cart. They wouldn't fit. We had to have Steve "Swizzle Stick" Shelman ride along. He was the night bartender at the Indian bingo parlor in Bonsall. He weighed about the same as Don Knotts, and his ex-wife, "the Twirl," looked like a piece of loose wire standing vertically. They would make a "fitting" foursome.

We had a late withdrawal and were short two antagonists. Joe, the club manager, was walking by and heard of our dilemma. "If you want, I can grab one of the girls from The Baby Doll House and bring her as my ex. She'll probably end up as my former anyway!" We all thought that was a good idea, and besides, Dawn had huge snap-ons she paraded with no discretion. What a tournament.

After two and a half hours of changing lineups, we all agreed on the pairings of the four foursomes. It was one hour to critical mass and the ladies were starting to arrive. They arrived in their ex's former cars. The guys would sneak out and take a look at their former real property. Most of them were misty-eyed as they walked back into the double-wide to pay their greens fees. That was one of the rules, each participant had to pay for himself. We had already paid enough.

I would stand by the register and watch Head Pro ring up the fees. You could tell if one of the guys thought he might get a romp in the rack—he would pay for hers. I, of course, would spread the news. The guilty were met with cries of "scum-sucking traitor dogs" by the male participants. This was male social bonding.

There was a list of five rules that had nothing to do with the play of the tournament. They were more legal in nature.

1. No guns or sharp instruments were allowed in the golf cart.
2. Women could not allude to the size of your dick during the course of your golf swing. Any other time was appropriate.
3. You may never talk about the "real" reason for your divorce. Either party.

4. Current "boyfriends" or "girlfriends" were not allowed on the premises.
5. There was a standing eight count for any fighting between couples.

The $22 tournament fee included nine holes of golf with cart. One drink, and a festive dinner, Cold Duck, and a quiet evening at the Mike Tyson Combat Dance shortly after conclusion of play. Two hole-in-one prizes were donated by the club. If a woman made a hole in one on the sixth- or eighth-hole par-3s, she would receive a two-day cruise on Club Med to Cabo San Lucas with a Chippendale dancer of her choice. That is why we had such a large turnout, by the former spouses, for the Ex-Wives Conflict golf tournament.

If a man made a hole in one on the sixth or eighth hole, he would be allowed to get back any piece of real property that he lost in the divorce, except the former house. The women agreed to this because of the Chippendale deal, and because the last time their former husbands had made a hole in one was when the Dead Sea was just sick.

There was a prize for the "farthest" away on the par-3s. For the ladies, it was a $20 gift certificate for costume jewelry at Wal-Mart.

For the men, two free "lap dances" at The Baby Doll House entertainment club. There was a lot of mis-clubbing going on due to the nature of the prize.

The tournament began without incident, unless you count the kidney punch that The Breathalyzer's ex, Noreen, threw at him when he asked her, "Is that your cleavage or a scar from your open-heart surgery?" It was ruled a clean punch.

The cocktail cart was huffing and puffing around the front

side, trying to keep all participants focused. Nadine, the cocktail cart queen, was a dropout from the local university. She had a constant frown and a world-class body. The ex-wives blamed her for most of the divorces.

Worst-ball format with your ex-wife can take a lot out of you. It is insufferable in duration and endless in pity. Scores of seventeen and twenty-one were posted on the first hole for worst-ball, and they were the lowest scores. The afternoon raged on with the speed of a marauding glacier. Tempers and four-irons were flaring. Most of the ex-couples now remembered why their marriages were dissolved.

All in all, it was a pretty peaceful day. Mad Max said he lost control of his cart, as it narrowly missed his ex, Tanya, and careened into the lake on nine. After rescuing their bags from the sunken cart, Mad Max was heard to say, "If it only had rack-and-pinion steering, I could have had her!" The rest of the day went without incident.

After a brief cocktail party, where we exceeded our one-drink limit, we all sat down for the entrée. I noticed a commotion at one of the tables and then everybody in the room was starting to giggle. The Breathalyzer said, "Look at this menu." I picked up mine and started to peruse.

Under appetizers, it read:

Cream on a Cracker—Just about anything and cream cheese is wonderful. $5.50

Faggie Funghi—These slippery little marinated mushrooms are great to roll around on your tongue. You might say they're a limbering-up exercise for the main course. $6.25.

Under soups, it read:

Bitchyssoise—Basically, this is a bitched-up cucumber soup.

It has, however, enormous soothing properties. When I'm in one of my bitchy moods, this pulls my fangs back in. $3.50

Under salads, it read:

Chicken in the brown—Certain to get your cock crowing. $4.50

Under entrées, it read:

Beat your Meatloaf—A truly sensual way to dispose of two pounds of ground round. $10.50

The Seaman's Rod—Set sail for an adventure in eating where men are gay in swashing their bucks, and buckling their swashes. The taste of this dish will have you coming about in no time. $12.95

What kind of menu was this! San Francisco takeout? As the dining room was laughing hysterically, I noticed two derelicts engaging in light conversation at the bar. It was Packy and Muzzy, the poignant pranksters. They had a stack of menus in front of them and were showing the forgery to Quick Pour, the bartender. Seems that the boys got bored over at the paddocks one day and were reading this gay recipe book they had acquired from Chez-Juan. They decided to steal a menu from the dining room and have it forged and replaced with sixty new menus of the "light cuisine."

The Cold Duck was served and most of us were getting cold tongue from our ex-wives. The band, Los Gringos, was playing up a storm and the Mike Tyson Combat Dance had begun. There was plenty of slow dancing and long embraces as the whiskey dulled our senses. Tears of misgivings were walking slowly down the cheeks of former spouses. There was back alimony in the air.

Finally, well into the night, Head Pro announced the losers of the Ex-Wives Conflict Worst Ball Golf Tournament, Mad Max and his lovely ex, Tanya. As is customary, Los Gringos played Frank

Sinatra's "My Way," as the former couple had to read, word for word, their final divorce decree. It brought tears to the eyes of the audience, as everyone got maudlin. We combat-danced the night away and finally all of us made our way out the doors into the shimmering night. As we stood together, ex-spouses united by golf, and looked at the dead palm tree silhouette against the San Diego full moon, we could only surmise it must have been Muzzy and Packy who had let the air out of all the former wives' car tires. What a tournament!

Blindman's Buff

Most of us play golf for one reason: to bet. We don't play it for the sunshine, we don't play it for the exercise (for proof, take a look at Ben Wright), and we surely don't play it for relaxation. Most of the guys I play with need a clinical psychologist and a straitjacket. We play this game to gamble with our buddies and try to beat them into Chapter 11.

At the muni golf course where I played a lot of golf, all my derelict buddies circled like vultures around a dead carcass. As you know, this place is called the Downs. If you wanted some action, this was the place to loiter. Jimmy the Greek should have been a member there.

This place really does exist and I get back there as much as possible to steal some more lines for TV. I don't know many of the guys' real names because we always used nicknames. That way if their wives called looking for them, we could honestly say, "I'm sorry—we haven't seen Bob Tucker," because everybody but his wife knows him as Fairway Louie. My Christmas card list was great. Besides the people you have already met—The Kitchen; Brain Damage, Unemployed Lloyd; Colonel Klink; my guru, Fairway Louie, who taught me about life; and Mad Max, there was Moon, the Rodent, Lex Luther, El Gato and the Three-Legged Dog, London Sam, and the Grave Digger (he took deep divots). They all had phony handicaps. They are my friends.

This one particular day, after some serious male bonding on the golf course, we were in an extra-innings gin game when a blind guy walked into the adult beverage room wielding a white cane with a red tip. We immediately addressed him as 20/20. Two of my buddies shot out of their seats and confronted the gentleman, wanting to know what his handicap was and if he ever played from the back tees. He said it didn't matter which tees he played from, as long as the match was at night! He sounded like one of the guys; he sat down, and joined the boys at gin.

I immediately ginned and excused myself to go down to the drugstore, where I found everything I needed: cotton, duct tape, an Ace bandage, a black sack with a drawstring, and a Johnny Mathis tape. I didn't forget a thing.

I rushed back to the Downs and found Mad Max. He had the perfect personality—he would do anything for money. He was a Vietnam vet who used to deliver pizzas to Cambodia. He drives very fast.

The bet was simple: Mad Max had to walk, blindfolded, from the tenth tee and touch the flagstick on the green in less than thirty minutes. I used all the stuff I bought at the drugstore to ensure his darkness. A substantial amount was bet he could not complete the task. Mad Max took all the action.

So a cast of forty or so tank-topped, cart-pulling sandbaggers and assorted barmaids went out to the tenth tee and watched as I blindfolded Mad Max. I acquired a ghetto blaster to drown out any familiar sounds—Johnny Mathis will do that—and spun him around five times and off he went.

The tenth hole has an elevated tee, and a fairway with a creek on the left and a lake on the right. There were two dead trees up by the green. One of the cocktail waitresses was pregnant. There was excitement in the air.

The first move by Mad Max was perfect—he fell off the front of the tee and rolled into the creek. Our bet was looking good. Unshaken, he got up, found the cart path that went to the lake, and followed the shoreline. Other than two slight miscalculations where he turned too soon and walked into the lake, he was doing fine. A little wet, but fine. Toward the green he went. Only one incident involving his forehead and a palm tree interrupted his flight to the green. He made it to the green in twenty-two minutes. The hole is only 367 yards long, but it never played tougher.

He had less than seven minutes to touch the flagstick. Arms outstretched, he wandered the green searching for the elusive flag; with two minutes and thirty-two seconds left he made a rumblin', bumblin', stumblin' turn and walked into the flagstick and immortality. It was better than winning a major. At least that's what he said in the acceptance speech.

We were giving Mad Max his money and about ready to evacuate the premises when 20/20 came riding up in a golf cart, causing the crowd to disperse immediately. He said he heard about the bet and that he could do it in ten minutes without using his white cane with the red tip. We said no bet and took him back to the gin table.

The Scramble

The buzz around the Downs was that a famous writer was coming in to do a real live story on my pathetic career, and he wanted to see firsthand where I displayed my ineptitude on a daily basis, and get to know my warped friends. It was in the late eighties, and the boys were in a frenzy at San Luis Rey Downs thinking they could get their picture in the Bible of golf publications, *Golf Digest*. It was like Ed McMahon was coming to town to award them the first prize in the Publishers Clearing House Sweepstakes contest. There were people running everywhere. They had all their best-looking outfits on, old clothes that I had given them from the Tour. They were all looking like a Munsingwear ad and were ready to get quoted.

I picked the writer up at the airport in a late-model foreign convertible that was just about paid for. I even washed it. We exchanged pleasantries and I informed him we were going to the course and play some golf with the local denizens of this muni madhouse. He didn't have his clubs with him, so we stopped along the way at Escondido, California's finest storage facility, where I had just spent the night counting mice crawl over my cot. It had a cozy feeling, my storage space (8′ by 10′), and all the amenities of a just-divorced bachelor. It had electricity.

He complimented me on the decor, which was early Titleist. We grabbed some clubs and off we went in pursuit of fame and fortune at the Downs. I informed him that these guys were a little left of the plumb bob and they might be a little eager to offer tales of my misguided past so they could get their names in *Golf Digest*. Most of the stories were made up, I told him.

We arrived at the course, and it was as busy as Ian Baker-Finch looking for his ball. The boys were all gathered in the modular that was supposed to be a temporary clubhouse eleven years ago. It had that mobile-home-park atmosphere that would be hard to replace, so they just put flowers around it and called it home.

It was announced over the PA system, the one we stole from Jack-in-the-Box last winter when they were under construction, that everybody was to meet on the first tee at high noon for the choosing of the teams. There were twenty-five players involved; we chose the five best players as the captains and they drew numbers to see who chose in what order. The captains were Fairway Louie, Reilly "the Tin Man" Robinson (he had no heart), me (I was one of the best players in this group), and two former veterans from foreign wars, Mad Max and Lex Luther. In that order.

As the captains stood on one side and the rest of the motley crew stood picking their noses on the other side of the tee, I could only think that this is what it must have looked like when Larry Storch was picking guys to watch the fort in *F Troop*. There was not a Ben Hogan among these guys.

My picks were real easy. The writer was a mandatory one, and because he was from Stanford University, I picked the brightest guy amongst the rest of the culls, Laboratory Lenny, who works the night shift at San Diego State. I wanted the writer to feel intellectually stimulated during the round. Laboratory Lenny tells everybody he works in the physics lab, but he's really the night custodian. That's the closest guy we have to an intellectual and the closest thing we've got to a guy who has seen a college.

My last pick was a shrewd one. I picked "The Bear," a former Red Sox catcher who has two bad hips that are going to be replaced. For now, he hobbles up to the tee with his crutches and then drops them before he hits the ball. Then he picks his crutches up with his club and stumbles back to his cart. The Bear weighs 312 pounds with his crutches, so I have him walk in somebody's line just before the guy putts. The guy would have a better chance of dating Elle Macpherson than making that putt.

The game is this: We tee off with twenty-five guys, five five-man teams. It's a Scramble event playing the best shot of the five, and there is no order on the tee. Everybody hits when they get some room. The bet is $50 per man for the lowest nine-hole score. So that's $200 per man for the winning team. The cart girls have halter tops on, exposing tattoos, and they are selling beer for $1. There's excitement in the air and the insults have started.

Nothing noteworthy really happened until the sixth hole, when the team we were tied with missed a three-foot birdie putt because The Bear stuck one of his crutch marks right in their line and they missed the putt. After The Bear had hit his next tee shot and was crutching his way to the cart, the guys did a drive-by and knocked the crutches out from under his arms, and The Bear fell on his Red Sox ass. Laboratory Lenny just about puked, he was laughing so hard. What a group.

The last hole is a par-five with a toxic river running parallel left to this hole. We were tied with Lex Luther's group and both teams had thirty-footers for eagles on the hole. There was a chill in the air as everybody in the clubhouse was watching this experiment in social dysfunction. We lagged our putt down the slippery slope of grass and dirt to about four feet and made the putt. Lex's team was not so fortunate; the best they could do was ten feet. Three of his teammates were dropouts from the Betty Ford Clinic and their putting strokes resembled Orville Moody's.

It got down to Lex having to make the ten-footer, as all his neurally afflicted teammates had given their putt the Ginsberg and he was the only one left as the sun was setting. Lex had spent some time in "the rice field country club," as he called it. Vietnam, as we know it, and I'm sure he ingested some foreign chemicals while he was there, because he was a couple balls short of a dozen. When he missed his putt by coming up a foot and a half short, all hell broke loose. He went screaming and running to his golf bag. We all hit the deck because we knew he used that bag as a rifle rack for his Uzi. He opened fire on the roof of the clubhouse as everybody took cover. It looked like a scene from an Arnold Schwarzenegger movie.

When the clip had emptied and the smoke from the Uzi was wafting toward the evening sky, two illegal aliens came up from the toxic river, where they had been hiding, holding their hands high in the air in surrender. They thought U.S. Immigration had found them out. They walked calmly toward Lex, hoping he wouldn't shoot them and cause an international incident.

As we all started toward the shot-up clubhouse, Lex was trying his damnedest, in broken Spanish, to convince these guys that he was not the law and that soon the law would be coming for his young ass. As the police sirens were wailing coming up the road, we all looked through the clubhouse window and saw Lex leading his two new friends into the toxic river to hide.

The next big argument was who was going down into the toxic river to get Lex's $50. Reilly "the Tin Man" Robinson said he would. He had good training in these sorts of things, he was a U.S. Immigration officer. What a group.

The Cocoon of Flight

"The purgatory of my inane inefficiencies with a golf club spells doom for the flight of the ball."

—G. McCord

When a golf ball is tossed through the air toward your caddie to clean, the flight is parabolic, or rounded. There is not much force acting on a ball going that slowly. But if you hit a ball like John Daly does, it travels at speeds up to 180 mph; the force of the air on the ball is not small. This force, in a lot of cases, can become even larger than the weight of the ball and can produce some spectacular modifications in its flight path.

In Zen, they have the three evil paths: the realms of hell, hungry ghosts, and beasts. I have seen them all with my golf ball. I now must find that path to seek the sanctuary of the fairways. If there is one line that has been spoken that tells of the true Zenlike qualities of golf, it was Chevy Chase in *Caddyshack*, when he said, "Be the ball, na na na na, ne ne ne ne." A clever mantra.

I will start this journey with a story about my spiritual guide, Mac O'Grady. I got the phone call at 7:15 A.M. in my motel room in Hartford, Connecticut. I was there for the Greater Hartford Open Golf Tournament, working for CBS. The call from Mac was not strange because of the hour, but for the content. He expressed to me that he had had another vision and had woken up at 2:15 A.M. He'd gotten a drinking glass, a candle, and a golf ball. He proceeded to put the ball on top of the glass with the lit candle behind it. In a lotus position, he stared at the ball for four hours and fifteen minutes, until he got "into" the ball. It must have worked, because he won the golf tournament. What an interesting concept. Get into the ball.

Seeking the ultimate flight, I got the necessary resources for my flight: a launcher, Fairway Louie (the Men's Club president at San Luis Rey Downs. Long but wrong), a three-piece Titleist Professional 90 compression (didn't want the 100s, they're wound too tight), and a map of how to get back out if I got in!

The instructions were to play the "Jack Daniel's Loop" at San Luis Rey. Holes one, seven, eight, and nine. They had everything. Traffic on one side and swamp on the other. I used the head professional's office for my metamorphosis, and the snack shop girls were ready for the overflow from this daring feat.

I told everyone in the modular home used as a pro shop that they should check on me in three hours to see if I had in fact gotten into the ball. If I was gone, I must be in the ball and to carefully place me on the tee and let Fairway Louie give me a launch. Louie was confined to his room three days in advance and not allowed any outside stimulus. I was ready for this transformation. Mac had given me all the instructions.

The day was calm, with a slight overcast from the ocean, when I entered the pro's office. It acted as my "Zendo," or large hall, for Zazen. Fairway Louie was there with a ninja headband on that said, "Grip it and rip it." Oh God, was my launcher already launched? Too late now. I am in my semi-lotus position staring at the ball, back-lit by a used candle they found in the starter's shed. I was ready for my hibernation in the womb of rubber bands.

"My intention is to tell of bodies changed to different forms." Ovid, *Metamorphoses*.

The light was constant in the room and my focus on the ball was centered. I picked out a speck in a dimple that was a flaw in this illuminating white sphere. After a while, I don't know how long, my body was being sucked into the orb. The quiet meditation had produced a phototropic response, and I was now inside. I was light, I was trapped, I was free.

I pried my way around inside this three-piece ball until I found the center. I don't know how small I had become, but I was small enough. I found the liquid center of this sphere and sat down. My eyes saw nothing, but I felt confined within my own realm, and I was ready for clueless flight.

I felt somebody lift me up from the glass and walk for about three minutes. I was on the first tee. I waited with wild anticipation for that first nuclearlike collision. The force that I felt from the backside was incredible. Luckily, I was facing forward, sitting on the liquefied center, and I was about to experience Newton's first law. The collision produced about three thousand pounds of force and the ball flattened behind me and through the conservation of momentum. I was launched at the speed of about 145 mph. Left.

Off the horizontal axis, I felt a dip below the parallel on the left side. I was blind-riding in my wayward tomb, and Fairway Louie said he wasn't playing very well. I felt this sudden deflection, and then my internal organs proceeded, as my skin drew taut, to stop their momentum. I had landed. Probably in the cottonwood trees to the left of the fairway. He's called "Fairway" Louie because he doesn't hit many. But I wanted a wild ride, a class-five rapid.

The thought of the second shot was wild, as I tried to predict what shot he was going to have to hit and when I would be launched. Great adrenaline rush. Thank God I was wearing dark-colored Fruit Of The Loom underwear.

I was suddenly whacked and rolling along the ground, bouncing like I was a bowling ball with a limp. I don't know if he'd topped me, or if he was playing a bump-and-run shot. I must have been topped. Fairway can't hit a bump-and-run.

I finally came to rest in a cushioned landing. Probably in the front left bunker. The bunkers at San Luis Rey don't have much sand, so I hoped Fairway wasn't going to hit a "Vince Scully" and tear out my spleen. The impact was wild. I felt no club contact the ball, but I suddenly rose up like I was levitated by a magician. The softness of my being was extraordinary. I plopped on the ground with a few soft bounces and wondered how close I was to the pin. I heard a soft nudge to my right and rolled over gently, like the last three revolutions of a dryer after you've turned it off. I felt no falling sensation at the end. Fairway must have missed!

Off to the next tee, the seventh hole. Dogleg to the right, dead trees left, and a few live trees right. Second shot was a short iron to a poa-annua-infested green. I love this course. I was launched with an explosion from behind. My horizontal axis was tightly defined. A straight drive. A spinning golfnaut I was. Free from sight but anticipating a sudden crash. An early Russian cosmonaut must have had the same trepidation.

The crash to earth was soft and mushy. Must be the under-repair that is always in the driving area. A sewer leak from the five condos that decorate the left side of the fairway has never been fixed. It's part of the personality of the muni course.

The second shot was launched with a high rate of spin. Warning of a short flight. I actually felt myself back up on the green. Fairway Louie has never backed a ball up. He must have gotten one of those new square-grooved sand wedges. Must have been hunting around the lost-and-found lately! Two putts and I fell without fanfare five inches into the plastic cup. Fairway was on his game.

I had had enough. This constant spinning was giving me a balata headache and I reached for Mac's instructions on exiting this orb before Fairway Louie could get to the par-3. There was water left!

I took out my pen flashlight and reached for the instructions in my back right pocket. I pushed aside a few rubber bands and shined the flashlight on my escape directions. Mac O'Grady has never had much of a sense of humor, and I don't know why he chose this time to come out of his mirthless coma. The instructions were very clear and to the point, if you could understand Japanese. Mac and his wife, Fumiko, must have stayed up all night translating my escape directions into Japanese. They must still be laughing at my predicament. Trapped inside a golf ball, owned and operated by Fairway Louie.

I will spend my life spinning on a horizontal axis at the muni, hoping one day Fairway will skull this thing bad enough so I can escape through the gash and tell of my metanormal experiences confined inside a turbulent and very elastic smaller earth.

Fear and Loathing on the Eighteenth Hole

Tour School

The final tournament of the year is the Tour Championship at the end of October. Golf's enema.

The march starts early in your mind if you're a skittish fringe player who dabbles in paranoia. It might take place on the early West Coast swing of the PGA Tour schedule. When most players are looking for that bolt of confidence to sever their brain, there is that fringe fraternity that deals in doom and gloom. The last thing a player wants to be is on "The Bubble" come the last tournament of the year. Various states of narcissistic pathology start to involve you. Players come out on the Tour and set different standards for themselves. Some come out to win, others come forth to exist. Neither should be judged. Both will evolve.

The Tour School is only ten months away. If I don't get off to a good start, I'll end up there again and lose what little sanity I have left in my feeble brain. I'm a denizen of the dread. I'm programmed for disaster. How can I be thinking about this now, it's only February third?!

What exactly is it that causes such fear in men? Why, when I asked Bruce Lietzke how he liked the Ryder Cup, did he respond with, "They were tight coming down to the end, but as far as pressure is concerned, I still think that playing in the Tour Qualifying School was the most pressure I've ever had. You only get one week for your career." You play that one week in November for your playing card and you couldn't suck oxygen with Mick Jagger's lips that week. I know, I've done it three times.

The Tour School is for those players who are trying to get on the PGA Tour, or have lost their card (playing privileges) and are trying to get back on the Tour. When I first got my playing card back in 1973, we had 370 players enter the two phases of the school, and twenty-three of us got our cards. We now had the right to go out and enjoy Monday qualifying.

The first Tour stop that year was the Los Angeles Open, where we had two golf courses with 180 players on each going for *one* spot on each course. Welcome to our nightmare! This is the most debilitating week you can spend on this planet if you chose this profession. The anxiety builds for months before in your pregnant mind. The self-ridicule, the paranoia, the angst. All these emotions are festering and gathering pace. Freud would somehow blame it on your mother.

You question your ability to play this game and question your very existence. Should I just quit now and go back to trade school or just go lie down? It is an emotion that exists in every one of us; some have it in their daily curriculum and others put it in the back of their minds to slowly fuse with their id and ego. The Tour School is Darwinian roulette. The strong will survive, but they will be seriously scarred.

One of golf's great iconoclasts, Mac O'Grady, and I played in the Tour School the last time I had to qualify. The year was 1983 and I was losing my zeal for this way of life. Mac and I were paired in the penultimate group on the last day. I had authored the All

Exempt Tour months before. This basically extended the exemption cutoff from the top sixty money winners to the top 125 players. In some sort of poetic justice, I lost my card and had to go back to get my card that year.

Mac had gone to seventeen straight qualifying schools without getting his card. He was very tired of golf's waiting room. Through some sort of mystical vortex, Mac and I got our cards that day. I wanted Mac and myself to go out to dinner that night and toast our good fortune. He politely said no, he had something to do that night. I saw Mac later in the year and the conversation got around to our making the school and how we each had celebrated.

I'd gone to a bar and had a few adult beverages, and Mac told me he'd gone to the nearest sporting goods store and gotten seventeen Louisville Slugger baseball bats, thirty-four ounces. He'd proceeded to take a Sharpie pen and scribe on the bats the location and date of every qualifying school he had missed.

Then he'd taken those bats, in the dead of the night, to a tree in back of the second green at the TPC of Jacksonville, where we had qualified, and broken every one over that pine tree in a primal ceremony. Welcome to the edge.

This is golf's version of hell week. We suffer from wounded self-esteem, shift rapidly from adoration to abhorrence and from grandiosity to the depths of despair. There is a shifting of mental imbalance. It affects our loved ones in the long run and our souls in this courtship of failure. I am a frailer individual for it.

The players who are entertained by this yearly massacre are probably the ones who will survive. They see moments when others see eternity. They are reeling in this domain of the strange, mired in self-possession. Survival of the finest.

I feel for these golfers every year at this time. They must prove themselves again. Some for the first time, others countless times. You can only go into battle so many times, then you decide on something else to possess you.

Their possession is their love for the game. Seek it until it deprives you of a life. "*Cogito, ergo sum* at Q school." I think, therefore I am at tour school.

Twilight Zone with Bubbles

"Start up the bubble machine."

I started this odyssey in the fall of 1973. The qualifying school was held in Pensacola, Florida, for seven holes and moved to Myrtle Beach for the final seventy-two. One hundred forty-four holes of sheer angst. About 560 golfers had originally signed to qualify, and there were sixteen spots waiting to be grabbed by the aspirants. I was lucky and played through the adrenaline and tied for third. Ben Crenshaw was the runaway winner by twelve shots. Now, twenty-three years later, the only thing I can remember is not going to sleep for the fourteen days prior to this emotional ritual. I was glad it was over and ready to embark on my new day job.

I had done very well in the mini tours and had saved a little money. The one thing I did not want to do was to spend my entire fortune trying to beat Jack Nicklaus. I had a wife and a five-year-old daughter and feeding them was a priority. Near Escondido, where I lived, was a mobile home park that was owned by Lawrence Welk. It had an eighteen-hole par-3 golf course surrounded by California live oaks and senior citizens. I don't know which moved faster.

The park was run by a family friend, named Paul Ryan. My father had played semi-pro baseball with Paul in the fifties. One night as they were regaling us with stories of past heroics, I came upon the idea of a potential sponsor. Someone who could open doors because of his stature in the entertainment field. Someone of charisma and cool. Someone who had his own TV show. Dick Van Dyke? Andy Griffith? Mort Sahl? Nah, too flashy, I needed someone a little more low-key, like myself. The answer was right in front of me. I asked Paul if he thought Mr. Welk would consider sponsoring someone on the PGA Tour. He told me he would look into it in the morning and give me a call.

As I was preparing to go practice, the phone rang. He had talked to Ted Lennon, Lawrence Welk's chief executive, and he was very receptive to the idea. A meeting between Ted and myself was set up for the following day. Financial security was just around the Hollywood corner.

I quickly forgot the golf practice and prepared a résumé. It lacked all the formal incantations, but I supplied many pictures to offset my lack of secretarial skills. I was pumped and ready to sell myself to the highest bidder.

I had no idea of what kind of sponsor arrangements existed in the free enterprise system of professional golf, so I called the PGA Tour office and requested any help they could give me. They supplied me with some standard contracts that had been negotiated by Tour players, and off I went into the study—actually it was the far end of the mobile home—and began to prepare my future.

Armed with two days of intense preparation, I made the two-hour drive to Santa Monica where Lawrence Welk had his office. I pulled into the monolithic structure that was located near the ocean, parked my car, and went fainthearted into the opening negotiations. I arrived at the fourteenth floor where the office was located, and poured my shaking body into the lobby. I was met immediately by the secretary, who escorted me into Ted Lennon's office.

Ted was a slight man with persistent eyes. He was sitting behind a huge mahogany desk that was backed up against a window that discovered the ocean. I was overmatched.

We talked for a long time and then started discussing the sponsorship agreement. He was using terms like: 30 percent of the realized value, interest payments on the loan, and personal service contract. Where was Ross Perot when you needed him?

We shook hands and I left the building full of doubt that Lawrence Welk and I were going to get together in an agreement. My champagne bubbles had been burst.

The PGA Tour is a dark, lonely expanse on your inaugural voyage. You don't have a clue where you're going or how to get there. I remember a story of a rookie Tour pro—I can't divulge his name because it *will* incriminate me. He had just finished playing the L.A. Open and was talking to a Tour official about the next stop in Honolulu for the Hawaiian Open. This Texan informed the Tour official that he would be late in arriving and where would be a nice hotel for his family to stay. "Many of the Tour pros stay at the Outrigger Hotel in Honolulu," he said.

"We're leaving tomorrow, how long of a drive is it?" said the rookie, with a faraway look in his eye. Life on the Tour can get complicated at times.

I had been to Carmel many times to play in the California State Amateur. I knew one thing: I couldn't afford to stay in "Carmel by the sea." I had not heard back from Ted Lennon, so I assumed my financial situation was my own. I checked into a dingy, traffic-ridden hotel in the main drive in Monterey. It had no phone but had Magic Fingers hooked to the bed. I was in vibrating heaven.

The opening round of the '74 Crosby was painful and cold. An Arctic storm had settled in and made life miserable for man and deer alike. Frigid rain was howling across the land and I was playing Cypress Point. That was like peering at a Rembrandt in a dark closet. Umbrellas were of no use, unless you wanted to re-create a scene from *Mary Poppins*. We all went slow and tried not to die of exposure.

I stood on the sixteenth tee of Cypress Point, a 231-yard par-3 that was biblical in stature, at thirteen over par. I glared through the rain and mist that was complicating my view and thought this was not the picture on the poster for the PGA Tour. This was my first Tour event and I was dressed like a shrimp fisherman in Norway, and I was standing on the hardest par-3 in our galaxy trying to par it to remain at thirteen over par. I was thinking I should have gone to law school.

I tried three times to tee my ball up in the frozen gale, hands numb from the cold and three-putting; I finally got it to stay and went into my pre-shot routine. The routine was to go behind the ball and shiver. Once the shivers had passed, I approached the ball knowing I was going to drown that shiny new Titleist in the Pacific. Burial at sea, I started to shed a tear for the little white fellow as I addressed the corpse.

From out of nowhere, Gordy Glenz, a Tour official, came riding by in his cart dressed like "Nanook of the North" and told us play had been canceled for the day. "Geez, can't I hit one more shot, I'm feeling a birdie coming up," I asked sorrowfully.

"Hit all the balls you want, I'm going inside and hug the fireplace," said Gordy, as he vanished in the mist.

"The birdie you're feeling is a penguin, and I'm going in," lamented my caddie. Disgusted, I picked up my potential birdie ball and followed my caddie to the clubhouse.

I went back to my palatial room and drip-dried everything, including my internal organs. If this was to be the start of my illustrious career, I was going to rust into oblivion.

The next day was thankfully better. The sun was shining and the seals were barking. The Monterey Peninsula was at its glorious best. I birdied the second hole and felt better flow to my golf. I birdied the seventh and the eighth and was breathing pure oxygen. The ninth, tenth, and tough eleventh fell to birdies and I was "smokin'." The siege continued with a thirty-footer on twelve and an eighteen-footer for birdie on thirteen! I had birdied seven holes in a row and was flush with the sweet nectar of good play. My karma was crankin'.

I now stood on the sixteenth hole at Cypress Point at eight under par and a convincing twenty-one shots better than the day before.

This is a stupid game.

As you would expect, I bogeyed the sixteenth and finished the round in 65, a two-shot lead on the field. A picture was put across the wire service of me missing a putt and a look on my face like I just had anchovy sherbet. I don't know where they got that picture, I don't remember missing any putt that day. Nevertheless, the exposure was overwhelming and about to tell a story.

I was applying the tourniquets to various parts of my body after a second-round 73 when the manager of the hotel knocked on my flimsy plywood door. "There is a phone call for you. It's waiting in the phone booth down on the corner."

"On the corner?" I asked with a furrowed brow.

"Yeah, there's a pay phone at the corner of the street; your call is waiting there."

I walked down to the corner and the phone was hanging away from its port. I picked it up and, somewhat chagrined, said, "Hello."

"This is ah Lawrence Welk, is this ah Gary McCord ah?"

I paused, looking for a candid camera, or some of my buddies on an adjacent corner. There was nobody in sight, so I answered the caller, "All right, who in the hell is this?"

"This is ah really Lawrence ah Welk. I saw your ah picture in the ah paper and I want to ah sponsor ah you."

"Damn it, who in the hell is this? Is this you, Fairway Louie?"

"My name is not ah Louie and I don't hit ah many ah fairways, this is ah Lawrence ah Welk."

It now dawned on me this could be Lawrence Welk. He has that same rhyming voice, and he is persistent. It couldn't be him, I'm on a pay phone in the dead of night with street people hanging outside the glass wanting to use it for their night's lodging. It was a twilight zone with bubbles.

After a strenuous cross-examination, I finally relented and convinced myself this was Lawrence Welk! What a fool am I. He told me that he felt sorry for me because of the picture in the paper. The look was so "distraught," as he said. I'm glad I didn't shoot 80 and they took a picture. If he thought I looked distraught shooting 65, he would have called the coroner for shooting the snowman.

He had talked to Ted Lennon and accepted the arrangement we had agreed on. "I want you to come on my ah show next week and we will introduce ah you to my ah viewing ah audience." I had played one good round on the PGA Tour and now I had a sponsor and was going to be on his television show. Only in America.

My wife and daughter accompanied me to the show. I was told to bring my golf clubs and deliver them to the set. They would have my seats in the audience reserved and Lawrence would bring me on during the course of the show. I was as nervous as Michael Jackson visiting the local YMCA.

There were about two hundred well-behaved, retired people crowding the room. Nothing much happened until they cut to a commercial and three cameras surrounded my space. Lights were blinding, things were happening, and there was show business in the air. The sign counted down, "Three, two, one, we're on the air!"

"I would ah like to ah introduce to you ah the newest ah member of our musical family ah Gary McLord." My God, he got my name wrong! No, I'm so nervous I couldn't understand him. Hell, nobody can understand him. What do I do now?

"Come up here, and let's ah hit some golf ah balls." As I floated up toward the stage, I noticed my golf bag was standing next to Mr. Welk's. There was an AstroTurf mat with a plastic tee sticking out from its weave, and the mat was precariously close to the audience. Stage right was a bull's-eye target that was standing on a six-foot pole. What the hell was going on?

After some greetings, Mr. Welk informed me that I should grab a club and hit "the bull's-eye ah." I looked at him and then looked at the target. It was about forty feet away, off to my left, and looked like the size of a gnat's ass. How in the hell was I going to hit that target without warming up? Better yet, how was I going to swing in this outfit? I was wearing a brown and yellow paisley shirt made out of 100 percent polyester. I was smelling like a New York cabdriver in August. Draped nicely over the shirt was a leather jacket that was on the small side. I had bell-bottoms on that could have hid

Ronald McDonald's feet and four-inch wooden heels on my shoes. My hair was down to my shoulders and I had cheeks the size of a pie plate. I looked like a flower child who hadn't followed the instructions.

I took off my leather jacket, grabbed a golf ball, and teed it up, wondering what club would have the right trajectory to hit the sign. Oh God, what if I whiff it in front of a national television audience? As I tried to focus on the target through the sweat, I looked directly past the ball at the audience. They were six feet away from me, staring up with foggy eyes. If I shanked this ball, I was going to eradicate half of Sun City. These evil thoughts were bouncing around my head as I pulled out my favorite club, the four-iron. As I started to waggle the club, I noticed that with my four-inch wooden heels on, my weight had been transformed toward my toes. The gallery in front of me grew pensive. I was thinking about El Hosel (the shank) and death on a large scale.

I took the club back and tried to put my weight on my heels to offset the shoes. I went very slowly so I could monitor my movements. I released the club early in the downswing so I wouldn't shank it and looked up in wonderment as I actually hit the ball! It was plowing toward the target and ripped a hole in the outside ring. I didn't care, I hit the damn thing. I was so excited, this could have been my greatest shot.

Lawrence looked at me and said, "Now that ah you have ah warmed up, hit the bull's-eye." I knew I could not hit the damn sign again, no less the bull's-eye. I immediately got the guy playing the backup accordion and persuaded him to take a swing under my tutelage. Fast on my feet, and Mr. Welk accepted the fill-in and the rest of the show went without incident.

If anyone ever got a copy of that tape and saw how I looked

in those days, I would be worshiped, in some circles, as the Anti-Christ. CBS would take me off the air immediately and my AFTRA card would be revoked. Don't try, I've checked, the tapes have been destroyed.

Lawrence Welk was a wonderful man. We had a great player-sponsor relationship for three years. He enhanced my life.

It's Just a Putt.
It's Just a Putt . . .

Nothing can be so tame as a three-foot putt, right? Kato could make one borrowing O.J.'s putter. But try making one on Friday on your last hole to make the cut. This electrochemical-induced movement suddenly becomes the hardest thing you have ever done. Let me illustrate for you this bizarre mental Ping-Pong match, and you'll never think it's easy again.

The place was Arizona for the Phoenix Open. It was late afternoon on Friday, while you're choking your guts out trying to make the cut. The cut was going to be at 142, even par. I was in the penultimate group. My seven-iron had landed in the middle of the green with the pin tucked right. No time for bravery, just two putts and get out of here and enjoy making the cut. If you make the cut, you play on the weekend and get paid. That's a big difference from not making it and taking it out on your rental car.

The first putt screamed to a halt three feet short of the hole. My brain and my body are not in agreement. The rest is what I can remember of my ruminations.

How seemingly innocent this putt looks as I stalk it from behind. Pretty straight, sunset to my left, I can't help but notice it out of the corner of my eye. I love the desert's sunsets. It lights up in orange flames and beckons a spiritual gaze. Ansel Adams must have felt the same surge. What in the hell am I thinking about? My brain has an itch, and I can't scratch it.

Man, are there a lot of spike marks between the ball and the hole. These things must look like tall pines to the ants. They look like headstones to me; my brain is starting to go to black and white, and my body is starting to reject itself, the metamorphosis is suddenly upon me. Quiet the mind, you idiot, you are taking this way too seriously! I now am in a squat behind the ball looking over three feet of straight putt. Or is it? Everything breaks to downtown Phoenix around here, and I haven't got a map. But I think it's over to my right. Do you think the putt will wander that way? I can't hit this putt easy and play it outside the hole; my nerves can't take that. I'll have to put the speed freak on it and tattoo it on the back of the hole. Don't want to hit it too hard, might catch an edge and spin out. Must put my goosedown stroke on it, and let it use all of the hole. Boy, these spike marks are starting to talk to me. I swear one just winked.

Money is not an influence as I think about the consequences of missing this putt. A steady CBS check took care of that. There is a certain amount of pride that goes with the territory, and that is a driving force. Another driving force is that my wife wants to buy new furniture for our house "because," she said, "it's decorated in early Fred Sanford." The plot thickens!

I have now approached the setup and am startled by the odd-looking putter that I am gazing upon. Where did that head come from? I thought I had a blade putter. This thing looks like an old wheel rim from a Desoto with a crooked shaft attached to it. I am now flirting with a nervous breakdown.

I just remembered I went to that putter seven years ago. Must be the first time I've paid attention to its profile. As I put my hands on the grip, I can't help but smell the sweat as it pours over the suddenly crooked grip. My hands feel like two crabs trying to mate. How in the world did I get like this? Is this how Tom feels?

I noticed now that my shoes are in desperate need of a shine. The wandering through the desert has taken its toll and the jumping cholla needles have made my shoes look like they've been acupunctured. I must call Foot-Joy and get some of those new saddle models that Davis Love had on today; they would look good with my new . . . What in the hell am I thinking about? My wife is about to buy a whole house full of new furniture, and I've got to make this stupid putt for my own sanity.

The strength to hit a three-foot putt is about the same strength you use to brush your teeth, but for some reason I can't seem to get this putter back from the ball. My mind is willing, but my body is as stubborn as a rented mule. It's very simple, all you do is concentrate on a small piece of grass in the very back of the hole, take the putter back slowly and square to the line. Smooth transition, and stroke it with an accelerating putter. Out of the corner of my eye, I see a vulture circling high overhead. The Indians would call this an omen; I call it bad luck. There is nothing left but to hit the stupid ball and the hell with where it goes. The putter lurches forward and the never-ending battle between good and evil prevails. It slopped in!

I eventually played very well on the weekend and finished in ninth place. The bad news is I didn't play near as well as my wife shopped. All that aggravation and I still don't like the new furniture!

Yin and Yang at Work Here

Pure folly in an age of diminishing expectations.

My world is full of turmoil. I have embarked on that great charismatic pilgrimage called the PGA Tour for the last four tournaments, and I have failed miserably in my attempt at fortune and fame. I have a simple job to do, namely, get a semi-white sphere into a hole that measures four and one-quarter inches across, in the most expeditious manner possible. I have failed with a certain distinction.

My game is in posthypnotic Tour trauma. I have played holes in inexcusable fashion; six over par for the last nine holes at the Bob Hope Chrysler Classic and six over par for the last seven holes in the Phoenix Open to miss the cut. If I had a sharp instrument close by, I would be bleeding even today from the self-inflicted wounds. On second thought, I would have probably missed and torn a hole in the ozone!

On the other hand, I have been brilliant at times. After I put a Hormel (see the McCordisms list at the beginning of the book) on a fairly easy chip shot on the sixteenth hole at Indian Wells Country Club during the Bob Hope and only moved it a few feet, I quietly told my caddie that I would not be playing at the Phoenix

Open the next week and to find another bag. I had eleven more holes to play and promptly birdied nine of them! Does God know what he's putting me through? I'm on the verge of total neural dysfunction, and I feel like a birdie/bogey Ping-Pong ball. I'm a crash-test dummy for golf!

This makes me reflect on the big picture. What sinister forces are taking my soul? I truly believe that yin and yang are at work here. Yin and yang mean literally the "dark side" and the "sunny side" of the hill, in ancient Chinese philosophy. They must have invented this game. A pre-existentialist writer, the novelist Dostoyevsky, said that the universe does not make sense. Try caddying for me one tournament and you'll know he was right. At this point I cannot sort out the light or dark from any one tournament round of golf I play. I keep hearing the music "Helter Skelter" in my ear.

The only answer is to forge ahead and try to get some order in this maze of chaos, and get out of my contemporary malaise. I feel my brain racing at straightaway speed, and the brakes are nowhere to be found. Yang, hurry! Find the brake pedal!

I haven't got time to sit and dwell on the long-term effects of my miserable game at this time. The simple fact is I have four tournaments to enter the zone. I cannot hitchhike on the interstate of the PGA Tour waiting for a ride in the zone. My car has to be ready and filled with gas. My id, ego, and superego have to be woven properly in the neural corners of my mind, and physically I have to perform like Michael. Not much to ask. So why am I in the final stages of denial?

The more I play this game on a part-time basis, the more respect I have for a guy like Bruce Lietzke, who plays only fifteen times a year and plays well. (Greg Norman plays only sixteen tournaments or so on our tour, but plays fifteen or more worldwide.) Bruce coaches his kids' baseball teams for the remainder of the year, and the Foot-Joys get a full coat of dust.

The one word I cannot spell right now is patience. I put way too much pressure on myself to perform now—to make every putt that I have, regardless of the distance or the severity of the slope; to put every drive in position to go for the pin; to super-nuke the driver on every par-5 so I can play them like John Daly. My world is full of perfection, and I'm a condom with a hole in it.

I can handle the yang, but why do I get nothing but yin while I play this game? I know the world is made of opposites: light and dark, male and female, heaven and earth, birth and death, matter and spirit, balata and surlyn. This is my dualism. Well, dual this, Confucius: I want to have my yang!

Okay. I'll stop whining. This is exactly how I have talked to my caddie for the past four fruitless weeks. Can you imagine having an overpaid Tour player/announcer complain about anything? I haven't had a real job since my paper route, and I now can afford some good, fake jewelry for my wife. Life is good. Yang has appeared, but if I play, yin will be right around the corner.

I have a theory I've been working on, when I haven't been complaining to my caddie. It is a paradox that relates to your golf game on a linear platform. It is in motion (hopefully). But at any given moment of its movement, it is either where it is or where it is not. If it moves where it is, it must be standing still, and if it moves where it is not, then it can't be there; thus it can't move.

With questions like this rummaging through the attic of my feeble brain, I must go and contemplate the forces that are at work that assemble yin and yang. Besides, the doctor wants to talk to me during my four o'clock feeding.

I think they are going to start me on solid foods!

No Cuts, Golf Carts, Just Advil

I'm too young to be thinking about this! I'm only forty-eight years of age! All of my body parts still work, and I watch MTV. How old could I be? I feel like I'm twenty-five and act like I've seventeen, so why do people always ask me if I'm going to play the Senior Tour? Do I look like I'm old enough to play now? Maybe I should have worn sunscreen. Sure, I could use a little surgical help "facially," and maybe my hair has the thickness of a seven-day-old rye-grass divot, but I can just wear a hat. So why are all these people asking about the Senior Tour? My God, I know Hootie and the Blowfish personally! I'm not ready yet.

All the people I know who are fifty years of age are old. I moved out of Palm Springs because I was getting an urge to buy white belts and white loafers. I'm making an effort. I'm not ready to get in a golf cart yet. I still swing an "X" shaft!

But the numbers don't lie. I have four granddaughters, I like to eat early, I haven't been able to stay up and watch Letterman in more than two years, and I visit the bathroom at least three times a night. My God, it's true! I'm getting genetically programmed for the Jurassic Classic Tour. Geezerville, here I come. Maybe Retin-A could help!

Here are the reasons I should go on the Senior Tour:

1. My golf swing was completely overhauled by Mac O'Grady after I quit the Tour. It might be fun to see if it works now!
2. Leverage for my next contract with CBS.
3. There's no cut.
4. I like to drive Cadillacs.

Here are the reasons I should not go on the Senior Tour:

1. I'm allergic to Advil.
2. I want to keep my subscription to *Rolling Stone* magazine.
3. The same guys I couldn't beat for the last twenty-one years will beat the Ben-Gay out of me again.
4. I could possibly take a substantial pay cut.
5. My wife would rather follow Freddie Couples than Walt Zembriski.

I will keep a close eye on the future and live life to the fullest before I get to the magic age of fifty. I will try to ride a cart for nine holes once in a while to "get the hang of it." It's going to be a tough decision, but I've got two years to struggle with it. So leave me alone until then. See, I've got the grumpy part down already! See you on May 23, 1998, if I can remember by then what this was all about!

Majors and Minors

A Tale of Two Opens

June is the month of trolls hiding in the fairy-tale rough of U.S. Open venues. The crisp sound of high-tech golf balls colliding off sun-battered fairways that are tighter than O.J.'s gloves and bounding into the oblivion of bogeys that reside in the photosynthesized-enriched rough of U.S. Open golf courses. This scene has been repeated since balls were stuffed with feathers, and the golf balls were not too good then, either!

This is the time of year when we sharpen our trusty 62-degree, Zen gardening tool, flip it up to the atmosphere sand wedges. Nothing is closer to our soul at this time of the year than that square-grooved trowel. This is the potion that we have to take to offset the greenside rough we can expect from the USGA and the gremlins that act out their fantasies of fun. The Tin Man has a bigger heart than these former prisoner interrogators have.

Once negotiated onto the putting surface, the real fun of a U.S. Open venue will begin. Putting takes on the difficulty of trying to figure out a Dennis Miller monologue. You see and hear it, but you don't understand it. The greens are usually so fast, instead of using a mower they use the Zamboni machine to freshen them up. A player never questions his ability to putt more than during the week after playing a U.S. Open. The USGA should put a gift certificate for Dr. Kevorkian in the players' packets when registering.

This form of terrorism is always reserved for the start of summer, and the players can't wait to see how their games stack up against this foe of tight fairways and maniacal rough. Nothing changes, and survival is a good book about thanatology.

The strategy of this kind of golf is choiceless. Individuals are thrust into existence for a short time only. Existentialist theologian Karl Barth called this "the boundary situation." They come into this world at a specific time, and they leave it at another specific time. About this there is no choice. This is what a U.S. Open is about. Drive in the fairway, play to the middle of hard greens, and hope to two-putt. Most golf courses we play in America are made to play with soft fairways and soft greens. The greens are bunkered accordingly. Then they stop putting water on them for the U.S. Open and expect the boys of summer to play run-up shots through bunkers to get at pin placements. Conservatism and the study of theology will help fight these forces of evil. The inevitable conqueror will be mild. Jones, Simpson, Irwin, Janzen.

The British Open, on the other hand, is a completely different venue. Played on courses that have been tested with the weather of time, they are built for rogue winds and undisciplined play. Dennis Rodman would enjoy a good British Open.

Many of our great players in the United States would not go over to the British Isles to play because, as they would say, it's a goofy game they play over there and not suited to our play. And, besides, it was a long boat ride in those days.

The game played over the pond is low against the wind and low with the wind. If it's blowing hard from either side, roll it along the ground. The courses are built for this game of "Bowling for Dollars." There are so many ways to navigate the ball, you will disconnect thinking about your choices. You folks without an imagination will not be allowed a visa.

The greens are usually voluptuous and have the movement of Superman's cape. But, strange over there, they keep the greens at a speed that can be negotiated by mere mortal men with putters. Interesting concept.

The lane is filled with heather and gorse, thistle and thyme. But it is not next to the greens where you can lose your caddie. The greens fall off into places of wonder and experiment where you can play just about any shot you can think of and a few Nostradamus couldn't predict. Former winners such as Watson, Ballesteros, and Daly can attest to freedom of choice. This is not a place for the culturally senile.

The geography between the two Opens is vast and the difference in style of play is even greater. The U.S. Open course's setup offers no choice for the golfer, just a paradigm of painful search.

The British venue offers more choices than the golfer can possibly deal with, and that is the essence of debilitating a golfer's mind. Make him choose late in the day when he has lockjaw of the brain.

In the words of the great French philosopher René Descartes: "I think, therefore I am." I think I would rather play in the British Open.

Between Planes

"Pass me the beer nuts, please. And who's winning the Open?"

Why does it seem that every time I want to watch the end of a major championship I'm on the road to an airport? I've got to get a new travel agent, or at least one who knows what I do for a living.

I am frantically driving down the mountain from Avon, Colorado, where I live, going through serious déjà vu from the same set of circumstances at the Masters this year. (Another major championship where I failed to see the extraordinary finish because I was on my way to the airport—nowhere near Augusta; they wouldn't even let me anywhere near the state.)

My life seems to be a succession of trips to the airport. Going to nowhere and arriving from over there. I can never seem to watch a major sporting event. I could use the VCR and tape it, but I can't work the stupid thing and besides, the slot on the VCR is where we hide our jewelry. When I arrived at the rental car agency, I called up three of my buddies to see what was going on with the U.S. Open, and they all told me not to tell them anything about the Open because they were taping it to see later, because their wives were making them work in the yard. Hell, I don't even know who's got the lead or how hard the wind is blowing.

It's taking forever to turn in my car, something about the right rear bumper not being there. Oh well, I better get to the terminal fast, there's not many three-putts left and I've got to find a TV.

Some good people want me to write a summary of the 1995 U.S. Open and they won't understand that I didn't see any of the last fifteen holes. Maybe I should do what I do on the tube and just make it up. Somehow I wish I could work that damn VCR.

I rush into the new mall they call DIA, Denver International Airport. I have no idea how far gate C-23 is, but I'm sitting down in the Prime Time Bar, ordering a tall cool beer with some stale beer nuts and watching the remaining agony the last four holes will bring to those in the hunt. The wind is blowing and there seems to be no friction anywhere. The golf balls are on Rollerblades!

The TVs are all tuned in to the Open, and the sound is barely audible. I'll have to rely on the expert commentary of all those around me. Most of the people are waiting for their lost luggage or late flights. There's excitement in the air, United just announced a gate change.

I'm dying to see a leader board, but the guy behind me in the Hawaiian shirt and velvet walking shorts informs everyone that Phil Mickelson is playing left-handed and asks when did he change. I wish they would turn up the sound.

I see wind dogging Greg Norman as he tries to flush the demons of the past with his new Zen attitude. His wedge to sixteen comes up short and he makes a funny face. The guy in the Hawaiian shirt is asking everyone around him when Phil Mickelson switched to left-handed. He gives up and orders another beer.

Meanwhile, the fiercest competitor we have on the Tour is

carving out what looks like one of those spectacular prime-time rounds they'll be talking about for years to come. Corey Pavin is one tough size small.

He appears to be playing the eighteenth hole. I cannot hear what the yardage is, but he has some kind of wood out. The guy behind me wants to know who's hitting and is it a par-5.

I said, "Pavin, and it's a par-four."

"What's he hittin' a wood for, then, if it's a par-four?"

I say, "It's his favorite club and he's tired."

"That can't be Pavin," he says, "he's way too tall. Hell, he's five inches taller than the guy he's playing with."

"That's Ian Woosnam he's paired with, and he's physically been lost twice in that rough left of sixteen."

He mumbles something about the beer being too warm and leaves me alone.

Corey hits one of the most beautiful four-woods I have ever seen, followed by a camera in the blimp. The eighteenth hole of the U.S. Open, a one-shot lead, and he dead-stones it at Shinnecock. It's going to happen to Norman again! They announce my flight is boarding. Anybody here know how far it is to gate 23? "Quiet," shouts an elderly woman eating nachos. "I'm trying to watch the Fish putt."

"Sorry, Norman is one of my favorites, too."

He bunkers the tee shot on seventeen as Corey pulls his five-footer. "Choker," two guys down at the end of the bar yell. I wonder what they do for a living.

I am now writing this summary of the U.S. Open only assuming that Corey Pavin finally got the primate off his back as being "the best player never to win a major." Or did Greg Norman finally beat destiny and hole a four-iron against the wind on eighteen at

Shinnecock, and send it into an eighteen-hole play-off on Monday? Yeah, right!

The year of the Bruins in basketball and now the U.S. Open. Congratulations, Corey, and I know most of the guys on the Tour would rather jump into a pit filled with mothers-in-law than play you *mano a mano*.

"Flight six seventy-three to Reno now boarding," cries the gate attendant. "Ma'am, I believe you're in my seat. Oh, by the way, thanks for spilling all that cheese from your nachos on it." Just another flight to nowhere, I'll be back soon from over there.

Cholesterol and Demon

Will you ever forget that four-wood that Corey Pavin hit to the last hole at Shinnecock to win the Open? As he raced up the hill to look at his just-launched sphere and the chills that gathered on your arms and down your back as he punched a hole with his fist, acknowledging his first major win?

The memories are clear, and the 1995 U.S. Open is nostalgia now. We move on to Oakland Hills near Detroit for another feast of fast greens and long rough. The pros will spill their guts and wax profane on this monster. The days are drawing near, the demons are gathering.

The fun part of the U.S. Open is the qualifying procedure that involves two qualifying sites to gain entry to the Open. When I was playing the Tour full-time, I only had to go through one qualifying round to gain entry. That was one too many. I have never been witness to the mass destruction that a U.S. Open can bestow on one's brain, I'm Open-less for my career.

The great thing about a U.S. Open is that anybody can enter, as long as he has a two handicap or less, or he can get a fake verification from a local pro at a course that has sand greens and three-wheeled electric carts. Usually these deals are negotiated at the local racetrack after a furious day of losing on the long shots, and the pro is more open to a bribe.

The quality of play is questionable, but the enthusiasm is there, and it has an odor. They gather for what we call the local qualifier in pursuit of the road to the Open trophy. They are long on confidence and short on reality. The Open champion will never emerge from this carnival of culls, but it is a good show regardless. I have been a witness to a few.

I don't remember the year, but it was well within my nostalgia. I remember flying all night from the East Coast to the West Coast. Poor planning on my part, but I was living in a storage shed in Escondido, California, at that time, and I wanted to get together with my stuff for a short while and try to qualify for the U.S. Open. I felt a victory coming on; I was still young.

I arrived late in the night and checked into a local Motel 6. The Motel 6 was my sanctuary from the norm at that time in my life. Besides, they had Magic Fingers, and I couldn't sleep without the stimulus. It was only ten minutes from the course. Thirty-six holes in one day at Industry Hills Golf Course in Southern California. It was summer, and the smog was omnipresent. I was feeling at home.

My starting time was around seven in the morning. The Magic Fingers left me a little brittle as I wandered to the practice area. Although I was on the Tour at that time (I wasn't high enough on the money list to be exempt from the sectionals), you never knew who you would be paired with. This was part of the lore of getting into the U.S. Open. I've played with guys who could give Charles Manson two a side for social dysfunction. It was a potpourri of fun, and you never knew what to expect.

I approached the first tee in anticipation of an arduous day of chasing my ball around this converted dump site, and the day got rather bizarre as I met my two fellow competitors.

Jim was the first fellow I was introduced to. He sauntered to the tee with combat boots, off-black and untied. Tank top, untucked over a pair of camouflage cutoffs. He had a headband that said, "Rules suck" and more tattoos than Dennis Rodman.

He stated he was playing a new Maxfli, number 3, that he found yesterday. "Good luck," he said.

I told him I was playing a Titleist 7, no cuts. "Good luck, Jim," I said.

Jim told me never to call him by that name; he goes by the name Demon. I noticed it was on one of his tattoos. Should be an interesting round, I thought.

The next guy wallowed up to the tee looking like he had an extreme case of gravity. He was 5′4″ and must have weighed 360 pounds. Jabba the Hutt must have been his father. He seemed like a nice guy as he extended his hand, and I shook it, jelly and all.

He went by the name of Cholesterol, and a few of his friends were with him to see him play with a Tour player. I expected to see Richard Simmons somewhere in the gallery. We showed each other what brand balls we were playing, and off we went in pursuit of the Open. I knew Cholesterol couldn't walk thirty-six holes if he was chasing a Twinkie, but I had to root for him; he was chasing his dream.

The Demon could really hit it a long way, but the confines of the course seemed to deter him from having a lot of fun. He talked to Satan most of the way around the course. I stayed on the other side of the fairway whenever possible.

Our only conversation on the first eighteen holes was when I suggested he should have the demonic code, 666, tattooed on his body. He thought it would be fun if we both got one. I told him I was a hemophiliac.

As his tee ball left him, so did the Demon's will to live. He had seven out-of-bounds for the opening eighteen and a score of 93. But the real fun was the fight he got into about a ruling on the fourteenth hole. He got real pissed off when his tee shot hit a cart path and bounced over a retaining wall into the superintendent's storage shed. He turned and made an awful face as he armed his club for an assault on the tee marker. The club came crashing down and pulverized the replica of Augusta National's clubhouse. The pieces went scattering, and an official just happened to be sitting in his cart a few yards away.

The local official told the Demon that he had moved an immovable obstruction, the tee marker, and it would cost him two strokes. The Demon had the dull stare of a dairy cow as he told the official he would find out where he lived. They got nose to nose and looked like Tommy Lasorda arguing with the third-base umpire.

One thing led to another, and one push ended up with the rules official getting knocked down on the tee with the Demon standing over him speaking in tongues. I looked over at Cholesterol, who was furiously eating a ham and scrambled egg sandwich.

The rules official got up and told the Demon he would see him after the round and settle this matter. You don't see this on the Tour much, I thought.

The rest of the round went on without another main event. Just a few more out-of-bounds by the Demon and a few occasional burps by Cholesterol. I was playing fast, just so I could see the confrontation at the end of the first round. My focus had been lost.

The round ended and we were met in the scoring tent by

every available local rules official. They converged on the Demon like bats on fruit. They told him to add two strokes to his total, and then turned to us to find out who threw the first punch. I told them I was helping Cholesterol get up the hill to the tee because his thighs were getting chafed, and he was having trouble walking. "I didn't see anything," I told them. I knew the Demon could find my storage locker if I squealed.

Before anything could happen from the rules officials huddled in the corner, the Demon started his scorecard on fire and then tried to light the scorer's tent on fire with his card. Cholesterol kept eating as Rome was starting to burn. I grabbed my golf bag and fled the tent. The fire was put out without much damage and the Demon was escorted from the premises by some police who showed up to handle a dangerous scorecard incident. I've never seen this on the Tour, I thought again.

I played the second eighteen holes without much distinction and without Cholesterol, who just wore out from all the excitement and chafed inner thighs. We said our good-byes and I liked his enthusiasm for the game. He was a good guy.

I played with two guys from the group in front of me who had lost one of their competitors. He had to go to work. So much for him winning the Open. I shot 72–74 and missed by a forward press. It took 144 to qualify.

Well, so much for me winning the U.S. Open that year. The memories of the Demon and Cholesterol will be etched in my frontal lobe for years to come, and the thought of winning the U.S. Open will have to wait another year if I can get by the sectionals and characters that fill this cauldron of chaos. This is golf's visitation room—come only if they're your family.

The Predator

The 1995 British Open is around the corner and I am wet with anticipation. Who could possibly win the ancient claret jug and walk on the old ruins, better known as St. Andrews, in proving his worth? Golf in its primal state.

My sanctuary has been the mountains where I live in the summer. High in the Rockies. No place answers the call for solitude and refreshment as does the rarefied air of Colorado. I'm a tracker, a mystical guide, and a window into the soul of the human spirit. I walk these mountains every morning searching for signs. I keep my eyes to the path and my nose to the wind. I am a tracker. I can sense the beast. I can read his dung. I have even tasted the scat left by many a fleeing mammal. Nothing goes without notice in the wild. You read every sign.

I decided to track that beast which is going to contend at St. Andrews for the British Open. I will use my uncanny abilities to stalk that creature, which I believe will have the brute pungent aroma of a winner. He may walk amongst you without revelation, but I can read the signs. My semi–Zen Master, Fairway Louie, had me read *The Tibetan Book of the Dead* when I was a young, inquisitive lad. I've been taught in the somatic verse since I laid down my first print. I'm now ready to stalk that polyester-clad day-feeder.

The best time to track is early morning after a night's rain. Make sure the moon was full the night before. It stirs the imagination. As the sun comes up, keep it at your back. Walk lightly as if you are a cloud with ballerina shoes on and wear no scent. This primate is very elusive and can backtrack you. Be aware.

Sometimes this golf predator wears wild clothes to show his manliness and sometimes he walks demure through the grass, giving nothing of his whereabouts. Evolution has made him elusive. He is a treat to track.

I start with my Sunday bag over my shoulder, minimal number of golf balls, and sundry items to keep the load light and the mind clear. Wet is the grass and the sun is to my back. The shadow cast is revealing. Nothing will go unnoticed.

The first track I encounter is Foot-Joy, size eleven, with one spike missing on the left toe. Toes pointing out indicate problems with hip flexors. Tight hamstrings are a problem with this individual. His stride is short. The footprints are not always going forward. They circle a lot, indicating this individual is looking back. He is not the predator but the prey. We will follow another set of tracks. This poor guy will be eaten by sunset. There are larger footprints starting to follow him. A swarm of them. It is a pack of wild, early-morning "I just made the cut" guys who are trying to make up ground. They are stalking the dew-sweeper. They will feed on his carcass soon.

As I cross over and start to play the third hole on this magnificent morning, I pick up the scent of pizza farts. As I come upon the tracks, they are toed out with the weight to the inside, or pronated. This indicates a knock-kneed individual who puts his weight to the medial, longitudinal arch of the foot. Not good for walking, an easy prey to stalk. I find a bunker he has just been in, tracks indicate not more than five holes ahead of me. The rake has been broken and the bunker unraked. Maybe a wounded golfer. Careful. They can backtrack you. All my systems are fully aware.

I come across some dung on the next hole and it's still steaming. The prey is close. The scat indicates this prey doesn't eat very well. Tiny bits of pepperoni mixed in with Twinkie wrappers. His food groups are found at McDonald's.

There are a number of towels along the way and parts of old *Racing Forms*. Clues, but I have to get a closer look. As I come over the hill looking down upon the green, I'm sure the wind is not to my back. I don't want him to get the scent. This formidable prey is lurking over a three-foot putt and he has just missed. Putter into the air and a stentorian bellow fills the morning air. Craig Stadler has been sighted. He starts to gnaw the aspen tree that is to the side of the green. He is definitely wounded and will not stalk any further. He will not contend at St. Andrews. Besides, there are no trees for him to put a towel underneath.

The next three holes there are no signs, only golf-cart tracks that end up underneath shady trees. Curious Ding Dong wrappers lie next to the golf-cart prints. An easy identification. PGA Tour officials.

The wind starts to blow and I have to be careful. I come across some footprints. Carefully measured, stride full of confidence. Tracks indicate weight on heels as he walks. Very proud. No deviation in his direction. He never looks back. He is a predator. There are some strange findings as I proceed. His tracks lead into the trees a lot and, finding some fresh scat, there are traces of ink in his dung.

I can't be more than two holes behind, and on the next green

I find the telltale signs of this predator's identification. Here his tracks start to become frenzied. Around the hole they become very deep, as if this golfer is thinking very much about what is to transpire. There is desperation in the air. A need for this short putt to get done. A neural load is to be dumped. It's Tom Watson.

If the wind blows all four days at the "Old Course," he will contend. If it doesn't, he will suffer. Hope all his ink stays in his stool and not in another letter about me.

As I come to the end of my day-tracking, I start to feel like I'm the one being preyed upon. How could this be? I'm in a mystical state and one with the land. Nothing can stalk the stalker. Yet I feel the steely eyes of the ultimate predator. I stumble upon the tracks and they scare me with their precision. Reeboks, I believe. Weight precisely secured from the Achilles tendon under the calf. A worthy adversary. He knows of the primal battle between being hunted and being the hunter.

The initial footprints indicate more weight on the right side as he walks. I do not know the meaning of this, but I keep my nose to the air and my eyes down. The adrenaline is flowing and my extrasensory perceptions are lit.

Footprints during the course of this predator's swing indicate a flurry of action. Left foot swivels left after impact, indicating massive hip movement. He is not hitting soft shots. His movement is ballistic in nature.

I come across some dung to the left of the eighteenth tee. He is very near. I can feel his presence. The scat indicates well fed, as the ultimate predator should be. His stool is thick, indicating a large orifice. A great beast is he. It also contains specks of wine. Opus 1, I gather. Don't ask. A better tracker there is not.

As I round the dogleg, next to a large lake 321 yards off the tee, there he is. Like a large bull elk rutting in the spring. The great white shark. (*Carcharodon carcharias*.) Going for this par-5 in two. Pin cut to the extreme left of his island green 279 yards over water. There is no doubt he will not lay up. "The Open" is his. He is in what they call mystical hibernation. He is awake but fully asleep.

Greg Norman is a formidable foe, but he reveals one thing in his tracks. The weight on his right shoe imprint indicates a heavy wallet in his right pocket. Does he play for the wrong reasons, or is this the reason for his predatory nature? Let's not analyze the wily creature. Let's enjoy his existence.

The Open is now over—and I have discovered that even the best of trackers can be put off the scent. As I stalked these worthy grass jockeys that were surefire contenders at St. Andrews, there came an unexpected conclusion. To win at this storied golf course, you need to hit the ball down, to be comfortable with golf low to the ground. Because of all the old aches and pains of this wrinkled old layout, a veteran would have the best chance to master the landscape. And, finally, a patient man would be the likeliest source to carve his initials in the claret jug.

John Daly did not fit this footprint. Yet he is the phantom of promiscuity. He is the British Open champion.

I hear the call of the wild. It is laughing.

The Masters

I was premature and in my incubation period as a golf commentator. The process had only just begun a few short months before, and my producer, Frank Chirkinian, had serious doubts about exposing me in such a grand theater. The year was 1986 and the entire CBS crew was having its usual nightly production meeting with full menu and discreet wine. The dialogue was as rich as the entrées.

We were feasting at the Tournament Players Championship, two weeks prior to the Masters, and the conversation turned quickly to who would be on what holes during the telecast in Augusta. Everyone had their assignments. Except me, who was left holding air.

I had only been working on a part-time basis for a few months, but there was excitement amongst the announcing crew that I was going to Augusta. When Frank excluded me from the fracas, anarchy prevailed. Pat Summerall led the charge for my induction into the mix, and the others followed. The heralding was met with contempt by our leader. I left saddened after dinner; the night and the Masters had seemingly passed.

It was late in the day on the Saturday telecast when Frank,

between commercial breaks, announced to everyone that I was going to the hallowed grounds of Augusta National after all. The serenity of my world was awakened.

I spent the week preceding the Masters at a friend's house in Atlanta trying to seek spiritual enlightenment. All I got was a call from my wife telling me she was seeking a divorce. So much for the spirituality of the moment, hello, alimony!

I was told to be at Augusta by Tuesday for a meeting with Hord Hardin, the tournament director. Frank was waiting patiently at our office for my arrival. We proceeded to Mr. Hardin's office; I felt like I was going to the principal's office. There was a look of concern on Frank's face as we went into the catacombs of the clubhouse at Augusta.

Jim Nantz joined us as we walked down the narrow corridor toward the door at the end of the hall. I was dressed rather spectacularly in my white Calvin Klein jeans, bulky DKNY sweater that was ablaze in yellow, the whole outfit topped with a Panama straw hat. I was a walking ridicule to tradition.

As we approached the darkened door at the end of the hall, it opened as if willed by a higher source. It creaked open as if this was the last time, and a shadowy figure appeared backlit against a ray of sun that filtered through the lone window. Hord Hardin greeted us like Lurch of the Addams Family.

Frank and Jim sat in the corner and I proceeded to take residence in the big couch in front of Mr. Hardin and his desk. I was the plot.

After some introductions and small talk about my work on television, Mr. Hardin proceeded to make a passionate speech about the flavor of this tournament. "We must maintain tradition, it is the cornerstone of the tournament," he said with conviction. It was a beautiful speech and actually kept my attention, which is hard to do. But I could not keep myself from looking around and seeing all the dimly lit pictures of Bobby Jones and the thirteenth hole that filled the room. It dawned on me that this was Augusta National, home of the Masters, and that this was a big deal. I was being circumcised by a green knife.

At moments like these, when I'm truly moved, I do something stupid. I think I do it because it relieves the tension, my tension. I waited until Mr. Hardin had made his closing remarks, and then abruptly stood up and asked him if he thought the clown outfit I was going to wear on Saturday was out of the question. Frank immediately put his head in his hands and Jim Nantz started to whistle.

Mr. Hardin looked at Frank, who was not about to look up, and then he addressed me. "Probably not a good idea."

"Damn, I'm gonna lose the deposit," I said, with my Panama hat pulled down over my eyes. It was a retort that Bill Murray would have been proud of.

As we walked out of his office and Mr. Hardin closed the aging oak door behind us, Frank reached up and grabbed the back of my neck and applied a pressure hold that would have choked a Burmese python. "Don't you ever just shut up and listen, you moron?" I couldn't respond because of the restriction of air in my esophagus, but Jim Nantz was faintly heard to say, "Maybe this is a bad idea bringing him here." Frank affirmed the notion with more pressure on my neck.

My next appointment, on my inaugural trip, was with my roommate for the week, Tom Weiskopf. We went over the entire golf course, and he showed me pieces of history as though they were paintings in his foyer. I could see his pride as he told me of past reflections, of his ordeals on this rolling green terrain. Augusta National was awakening his purpose.

My initial response to this rare edition of a golf course was totally sensory. I wallowed in the green of the thing. The color numbed my soul. There was social order everywhere. It was like a giant green operating room. There was no use for disinfectant. The ground and the air were pure in the springtime at Augusta.

The azaleas and dogwoods were the chrome on an old Buick. They shone as though nature's palate had absorbed a new intensity. The contrast of pine and intense color was mesmerizing. I was on a new level.

I do not remember much about the first few days of my maiden flight on the fourteenth tower. I was stuck into the trees on the right of the green and my allergies were on fire. I sat and had no idea what was ready to unfold on the back nine on Sunday.

As Jack Nicklaus started the back nine, he was just a participant in the story; others were center stage. But then, an eagle on fifteen, a birdie on sixteen, another on seventeen. He was now the only thespian. The others were experiencing mystical misfortune. It was as though it had already been written, and Jack was once again the show.

The trees were alive with communication. I can remember taking my headset partially off one ear so I could hear the sounds of triumph. They were deafening in their madness. The crowd carried him on the back of their exhilaration. It was nothing I had ever seen or heard before.

As the leaders passed my hole, I chose to sit in my tower and watch the rest of the telecast without the headset on to get a feel for the fun that was transpiring. It was really true about the voices of the autophones who take to this ritual of spring. They sing the praises of Nicklaus loud and clear, once again.

I remember calling Jack Nicklaus at his house three days later and thanking him for making my debut at the Masters a sacrosanct saga that will stay with me every spring, whether or not I am there.

But, of course, for the past couple of years, I haven't been there. The incident is now famous in song and story—the wee bit of irreverence in 1994 that got me expelled from the Master's Eden. For the record, here is what happened, as I wrote about it then . . .

There is an old Zen saying, "A calm sea does not make a good sailor." Does anybody have some extra buckets?

Over the last couple of weeks, I've felt like I've been driving on the San Diego Freeway in a slow white Bronco. The press is circling and the Council of Trent has made its decision. My ninth Masters as a member of the CBS broadcast team would be my last.

No debate. No bargaining. Just "McCord is outta here, if you want to stay, CBS."

I guess I should feel honored to join Jack Whitaker on the Masters blacklist. He is, after all, a man of eloquence and gentility whose only crime against the Augusta National regime was that he called a gallery that was running to get a better vantage point "a mob scene."

Jack's only regret was that he used a cliché and has to live with that cliché for the rest of his life. Jack's lucky. There seems to be no permanent damage. Twenty-eight years later, I can only hope to be as fortunate.

My problem is that I don't like clichés. Sure, I use them, but

I try not to. That's what got me into all this trouble. I have all this time on my hands, and I've got software in my computer that has a thesaurus. I wish I wasn't computer literate.

I constantly write material for my telecasts, trying to stay fresh and provide a little entertainment for my esteemed producer/director, Frank Chirkinian. I have made him an unstable life-form over the years, and for that I apologize. Frank has gone to bat for me on more than one occasion and was my chief defender in the Masters controversy.

I want to set the record straight regarding my offense, the scene of which was Sunday of the Masters. There is no better time to use a line that you have stolen from somebody than Sunday afternoon at the Masters. Everybody is watching then.

They came to me on the seventeenth hole when Jose Maria Olazabal was in conversation in Spanish with his caddie. I told the audience that I would interpret. I reported it this way: "Olazabal is telling his caddie that the only thing he doesn't want to do is hit it over the green. It's DOA down there."

Sure enough, he zips the ball over the green and it starts to free-fall down a steep embankment. I mentioned that if it rolls any farther it will be down there with some "body bags." He'll be dead down there.

Oops! My first rewritten cliché. He's dead. We use it a bunch in golf. He's dead. Don't know why we use it. Maybe it's the morbidity of the game itself. Stephen King surely has a knack for the game. His books suggest it. But back to the scene of the crime.

A few minutes later, Tom Lehman had a putt that was very fast. Being two strokes down at the time, he needed to make it. Time now for a line that would put into perspective how fast these greens are at Augusta National. That is the one question I get asked everywhere I go. It's topical. So I wrote some lines for the cliché "This putt is fast."

I came up with "These greens at Augusta are so fast, I don't think they mow them. I think they (a) use Nair on them; (b) use electrolysis on them; (c) pluck them; and (d) bikini-wax them.

Well, we all know that I used "d," and I'm outta there. Probably any of the four would have gotten me tossed. They gave me the Heimlich maneuver and I'm still choking on bikini wax.

In a world hungry for stink, this appears to rival Al Bundy's socks. There are stentorian bellows of foul play and censorship. Censorship is a very gray area when dealing with a democratic society, vague at best. In an autocratic society such as the Masters, there are no censorship laws. These people run the most prestigious tournament in the world, copied by all who view its efficiency and stature. They have got it right and they control it right down to when the azaleas and dogwoods bloom.

I applaud their decision. In the contract with CBS, they have the right to evaluate the announcers and decide who personifies the muted rituals of restraint. I am a loud wail. They are doing what they think is in the best interest of the Masters, and I can't argue with the decisions they have made to make this a near-spiritual gathering.

My only regret is that I put my good friend Frank Chirkinian and CBS into a position they couldn't win. CBS needs sports programming, especially the Masters. A business decision was made—we stay and Gary goes—and I stand behind it 100 percent. Frank fought long and hard for many months to save my PG-13 rating, and it must have taken a toll on him. He just punched himself out.

I have been asked whether being canned by the Masters will force me to change my style. Absolutely not. I was hired by Frank

Chirkinian to be Gary McCord. We're trying to put on the best event that we can and I'm going to do what I do—make it fun and bring the viewer a little closer to the sport.

I want to be known as a broadcaster who was a little different, started a new trend, made people look at golf a little differently. I'm not going to compromise myself. I'll continue to push the envelope.

Oops, another cliché. Where's that computer?

The Silly Season

"Hey, you! Over here!"

I looked in fascination as the carny called out to one and all who paraded by him. Calling for all to hear the fascination of something behind that tented door to excite and alarm the tender eyes of youth and the aging wonder of something that was dark and forbidden. Would you dare cross the line and explore that territory your mind said couldn't exist? You bet you would.

The golf year is over, and now we get to the silly season. Eight tournaments full of weird formats, corporate involvement, and plenty of cash. Welcome to the free money zone.

There exists on the Tour a time when our forty-two-tournament schedule is over. We start in early January and finally succumb right after the Tour Championship, sometime in late October. There is a lot of reflection, a post-posturing of just what to do next. Many Tour players lay down their implements and rest their weary brains, and many prepare to get really rich. It's that post-modern phenomenon on the Tour called Crazy 8s! Eight tournaments that are pitted against football for their ratings.

Quick! Think of something weird for a format. We play the whole year in stroke-play events. You find it and go hit it again;

everything counts. You, and you alone, to screw it up. I have had many long-distance telephone conversations with myself. Welcome to stroke play.

Now we can entertain any kind of format that looks good to the marketing side of IMG—Mark McCormack's ubiquitous International Marketing Group. Put your heads together, guys, and come up with the ultimate format that will set the Super Bowl back to leather helmets. It can't be that tough, the guys at home have never counted all their strokes in any of the weird games they play masquerading as golf. You guys at IMG, call Fairway Louie at his mobile home in Bonsal, California. He's got some strange formats, but he might be hard to find right now. He's cultivating his "crop" up on the hill. He'll be back after the harvest.

So this is what we have come up with: fifty-four guys going to lie in the sun in Maui and play for $1 million with no cut. Stroke play and all the mai tais you can drink. This is a great country. The PGA Grand Slam of Golf brings the four guys who have won the majors to Hawaii to play for a rude amount of money. John Daly driving par-4s in a hula skirt, and Corey Pavin meets the cast of *Baywatch*. I don't know about you, but my VCR is already set.

Then we have two players from each country meeting in China to find out what team can draw Peru early and catapult them to the winner's share of $1.2 million—aka, The World Cup of Golf.

The granddaddy of them all is waiting in Palm Springs. Four select players will be miked and entertaining you to the brink of nausea in the Skins Game. Sorry, *National Geographic* already has a special that day titled "Morphology of Subarctic Clams." I've already seen it once, but the ending is a thriller! I guess I'll miss another Skins Game.

How about getting a bunch of Greg's friends together, and have them play a format Fairway Louie couldn't conceive, and play for $1.1 million at the Shark Shootout? I wish Greg would invite me.

We've got left a tournament that you play with a member of the opposite sex, the JCPenney. Sorry, RuPaul, you'll have to find a partner from one side or the other! This is another tourney that involves teams from the Senior Tour, regular Tour, and the ladies' Tour. A potpourri of fun.

And finally, a new one that has been conducted throughout the year in match-play form from four different parts of the world, with the winners meeting at the end of December to decide it all for a $1 million payoff to the winner. The Andersen Consulting Match Play. Wow, Santa Claus on a global mission.

Is all of this nonsense good for the game? Should these players be subjecting themselves to enormous amounts of money in exotic places? Should the sponsors be putting all their money into tournaments that are outside the PGA Tour and going against football on TV? Are the golf tournaments at the beginning of the next year being hurt by all these stars playing in this silly season and taking more time off at the early tournaments? The answer to all these questions is, yep!

The Tour player is an independent contractor who goes where he can to make a living. I feel for the sponsors of the West Coast swing of the Tour. They have the best exposure for television and are having a hard time getting the stars to show up at classic tournaments like the Bob Hope Classic, the AT&T, and the L.A. Open. The show ponies are tired from playing in the silly season and waiting for the Florida swing to start. Besides, most of them live in Florida where there is no state income tax. Welcome to Paradise.

The Crazy 8s is a mutation of the game. They will live with us like dogs live with fleas. They are part of golf's food chain brought about by some bizarre Darwinian evolution. The sponsors are willing and the players will oblige. We're not rocket scientists out here, but in the words of H. L. Mencken: "We are a larva of the comfortable and complacent bourgeoisie, we are encapsulated in affectation and kept fat, saucy and contented."

Mo' money, mo' money, mo' money. It's time to go home, honey.

As the Season Turns

Well, the government is ready to shut down and Howard Stern is coming out with another book. It's appropriate that we are into week two of the Crazy 8s. The Shark Shootout is on the horizon.

A quick overview of just what has transpired with the silly season so far in this autumn of '95 should give us a read on what to expect for our coming attractions.

We started out at Kapalua, where as any good reporter would do to get into the story, I assumed the tournament lead early to get the flavor of our post-season madness. The flurry of television, the hounding of the press, and the insistence of the locker room attendant that I "must have cheated" put the whole carnival-of-golf thing into perspective. I started off the silly season with the lead! Where in the world are we going to go from here? Straight into the bowels of Comic Relief VII, I'm afraid.

The next journey into the center ring was the Grand Slam of Golf. This luau was in Hawaii, where the winners of the four major championships relaxed in floral underwear all day, sipping drinks with umbrellas in them and playing for a $400,000 first-place prize. Three guys—Steve Elkington, Corey Pavin, and Ben Crenshaw—

came to the last hole all tied. Ben hit a "Hawaiian Punch" pitch shot from sixty yards that would have traveled eighty yards, except that it hit the pin and went in for all the cash! Nothing silly about that.

The dreaded World Cup was next on the banquet table for your dining pleasure. Armed with three straight titles, our intrepid American representatives, Davis Love III and Freddie Couples, set out to China looking for human rights violations. All they found was a fourth straight win by a whopping margin and a country that should watch the movie *Caddyshack* to understand decorum on the golf course.

"Let 'em eat rice" were the words Freddie Couples supposedly uttered under his breath as he accepted the winner's trophy in front of four billion new Chinese golf fans. "Not one 'You da man' was heard," Freddie told me later.

That brings us to our next agenda item on the silly season platter, the Shark Shootout, where ten teams consisting of shiny names make their way through the floral elegance of Sherwood Country Club seeking fame and fortune in this dexter format. The first day's play will involve a Four Ball or Better Ball format. On each hole, each player plays through the hole using his own ball. The player whose score is the lowest on each hole will be counted as the team score for that hole. In other words, shoot for the flag if your partner is okay.

The second day's format is Foursomes or Alternate Shot. On each hole, each player drives and then the best drive is selected. The player whose drive was not selected hits the second shot and then the players alternate shots until the ball is holed. In other words, "Don't put your pards in the crapper."

The last format on Sunday is a Scramble. You all know what

that one is: on each hole, each player drives and the best drive is selected. Each player then plays a second shot from the spot where the selected drive lies and the best second shot is selected. This process is repeated until the hole is completed. This is where you want John Daly to be your partner!

The players love the Shark Shootout! What's not to like? The golf course is beautiful, the money is ridiculous, and everybody's far enough from L.A. to think we're not in L.A.! The locker room is something out of *Architectural Digest* with four attendants per player. There are enough Hollywood stars hanging around to make it an "event" and the food is free. What a country.

There are some show ponies playing this week, too! The team of Fred Couples and Brad Faxon are here to defend. The host, Greg Norman, and his steely-eyed million-dollar partner, Peter Jacobsen, have been at every Shark Shootout. The King and his court; what a trip! Fuzzy and Daly, enough said. O'Meara and Strange, what a year Mark has had. What a year Curtis has had!

This is a tournament that the players love. They like the goofy format and they like the lack of pressure. I like it because CBS is doing the broadcast and I'll be with Jim Nantz in the eighteenth tower this weekend. They don't let me up there a lot. I'm giddy with anticipation. Silly season is about halfway through and the Crazy 8s are rolling. It must be time to start my Christmas shopping!

Eight Is Enough

'Twas the night before Christmas and all through the place, there was only one more creature stirring in our season of the Crazy 8s.

The eight stockings were hung by the chimney with care, in hopes not another sponsor would appear.

There was the PGA Grand Slam and then the World Cup. The Shark Shootout from Franklin, and the Skins Game were up. The JCPenney Classic matched the men and the women, while the Father/Son Challenge left Office Depot grinnin'. Until, at last, the Crazy 8s were no more. Only the Diners Club left and then the Andersen Consulting to score.

The golf pros were nestled all snug in their mansion, while visions of huge guarantees danced with their passions.

And Mama in the Donna Karan and me in my logoed hat had just settled our bank accounts after a long silly season's nap.

When out on the lawn there arose such a clatter. Another sponsor was yelling. I said, "Hey, what's the matter?"

He sprang to his reindeer. To his tournament gave a whistle. There is one more to play and he jumped into his sleigh.

And I heard him exclaim, 'ere he drove out of sight, "Happy Christmas to all and to all a happy Andersen Consulting World Championship. Good night!"

At last, the last possible silly season tournament we can possibly cram into this Chinese year of the pig is upon us. The Andersen Consulting World Championship of Golf is coming to my house, the Grayhawk Golf Club in Scottsdale, Arizona. Peter Kostis and I have our golf schools here. This is the place we spread our word.

Let's take a look at this season-ending extravaganza. It began as a thirty-two-man single elimination match play consisting of eight players competing in four regional brackets: The United States, Europe, Japan, and the Rest of the World.

The original field consisted of seven players from each region selected according to Sony World Rankings. An eighth player was selected in consultation with Andersen Consulting. Players were invited to compete based on their end-of-year world ranking as of the year preceding the competition.

The regional competition took place during the spring and summer, with matches leading to regional champions.

The champions of each region will meet at the World Championship in Scottsdale for two semifinal matches, a third-place match, and a World Championship match. All matches are scheduled for eighteen holes, with the exception of the World Championship match on December 31, which is scheduled for thirty-six holes. The total purse is $3.65 million, with the winner receiving a cool $1 million. And Freddie Couples is not here?

The ones who are here met much earlier in the year, and they will bring their rusty games to Grayhawk this week. Mark McCumber defeated Loren Roberts to win the United States Regional and will play David Frost, who beat Robert Allenby. David represents the Rest of the World category.

Englishman Barry Lane defeated such show ponies as Bernhard Langer, Seve Ballesteros, and Sam Torrance to get into the finals.

Massy Kuramoto, who won three consecutive matches in Japan, will represent that region in the finals.

The PGA Tour, the PGA European Tour, PGA of South Africa/FNB Tour, the PGA of Japan, and PGA of AustralAsia all sanction this event. It is the PGA Tour's attempt to probe into the World Tour idea brought about by Greg Norman last year. I applaud the attempt.

The format is a good one, match play on a global scale, and the site is a friendly one. There will be good weather and beautiful surroundings. The sponsor is eager, $3.65 million proves that, but the time of the year sucks. We are bringing these guys from all over the world here during Christmas and New Year's for a world-scale golf tournament. It sounds like a CBS programming move.

For such a lot of money, there seems to be a lot of guys missing in action. Where's Freddie, Greg, Long John, Ernie Els, and the like? Did they look at the calendar for the finals? The chaos of the match-play format leveled this tournament on its inaugural flight to a less than shiny final four. A good scheme gone awry.

Barry Lane outdueled David Frost in this B movie, and walked out with a smile and one million dollars. Back to merry old England a little merrier. Thank you, Andersen Consulting World Championship, for your hospitality and a little less than desired final four. Welcome to the vagaries of match play.

"Now, Dasher! Now, Dancer and Vixen! On, Comet! On, Cupid! On, Donner and Blitzen! To the top of the porch, to the top of the wall! Now dash away, dash away, dash away all!"

And Then It Starts All Over Again . . .

Let me adjust my Titleist turban, look into my surlyn-covered two-piece crystal ball, and gaze into golf's upcoming season for some astounding predictions.

Let there be silence.

I predict Nick Faldo will be the one Madonna chooses to father her child and their daughter will eventually get a full golf scholarship to the University of Arizona to play under the new women's coach, Brenda Cepelak.

I predict that Ben Crenshaw wins the first four tournaments using a putter that's sixty-seven inches long and is later banned from the Tour when it is found out the putter he was using is actually the club-footed sister of Manute Bol.

I predict that Payne Stewart has his legs surgically shortened after his NFL apparel contract expires so all of his knickers can be recycled into long pants.

I predict that Michael Jordan quits basketball again, joins the PGA Tour, and signs a multimillion-dollar shoe contract with FootJoy and immediately loses his ability to jump.

I predict that the PGA, LPGA, USGA, and R&A merge and

hire Vanna White to be their commissioner because she's the only one who can figure out what to do with all those letters.

I predict that my embattled CBS sidekick, Ben Wright, is suspended by CBS from doing golf and is hired by the LPGA as an image consultant.

I predict that Greg Norman puts out a Christmas album sung by his entire family, but in a tearful press conference announces that it was a hoax and Milli Vanilli actually did the singing. The Norman family re-releases the album in Australia as a collection of "Outback Folk Songs." It does well.

In a bizarre scene, Hootie and the Blowfish buy all of the TPC golf courses so they have a place to play golf on their next concert tour of their new album *Fairweather Johnson*. Darius Rucker eventually falls off one of the spectator mounds, breaks both legs, and they have to cancel the tour.

I predict that John Daly makes so much money that he eventually buys a Las Vegas casino and has all the slot machines rigged so they pay off in M&M's. Hollywood eventually gets the movie rights.

I predict the Tour caddies' association puts together a video of exercises for the aspiring Tour caddie, complete with cigarette rolling paper, and it outsells the Richard Simmons workout tape. Ten percent of their profits are donated to the Colombian government.

I predict that Chi Chi Rodriguez actually stabs himself with his putter after doing his birdie dance and has to be hospitalized and kept overnight under police surveillance. The authorities think it was a suicide attempt.

I predict that Gary McCord wins an Academy Award for his

role in *Tin Cup*. He is eventually barred from Hollywood for overacting.

Corey Pavin is thrown off the PGA Tour because he could not maintain the height requirement.

I predict Mark McCumber quits the Tour and becomes an entomologist.

And finally, Prozac becomes the "official drug of the PGA Tour."

Off the Tour

In Search of Work

The year was 1986, and my professional goals and aspirations were making a house call on Dr. Kevorkian. I was awash in the urinal of life and limited success was now an exaggeration. The Tour was a vast, empty wasteland of setbacks and spent money. I was serving out the rest of my sentence with no chance of parole. Golf sucks.

As I boarded my airplane for Columbus, Ohio, nothing really was on my mind other than two fat housewives I was going to be sitting between in the economy section. I was in my customary hesitant gaze when I was awoken by harsh criticism coming from the first-class section. It was the CBS crew that does golf, and they were already enjoying the amenities of first class, although in a plastic cup before takeoff. Frank Chirkinian, executive producer and director, Pat Summerall, Ben Wright (the evil swine), Ken Venturi. All of them were basking in the knowledge that I was to be forever lost in the coach section wedged between two obese former fry cooks at International House of Pancakes for the duration of this flight. They told me I could come up here and use their rest room if I could peel myself from between the twin towers. I hope the front of the airplane falls off.

We were all going to Jack Nicklaus's golf tournament called the Memorial in Columbus, Ohio. We had just left Fort Worth, Texas, where I had played and CBS had televised the Colonial Invitational. I had just been elected to the policy board of the PGA Tour—the players elect three members of the Tour, and along with the three officers of the PGA of America and three independent business leaders, we make up the Tour policy board, which basically runs the Tour. It's a very important job for an idiot like me to have, but the players thought my life wasn't miserable enough, so they staked me to this tree.

I was going to Columbus not to play in Jack Nicklaus's tournament—it was an invitational and I wasn't high enough on the money list to buy a Big Mac—but to go to policy board meetings for the first three days of the week. They were closed-door meetings where I could usually catch up on my sleep. The next tournament was in Washington, D.C., for the Kemper, but I wouldn't have to leave until the end of the week.

I was fighting for a position on the armrest of seat 32B, when the flight attendant, a menacing-looking lady who looked like she was a guard in a ladies' halfway house for rehabilitating phone operators, came by and presented me with a bottle of wine, compliments of the royal family in the first-class section. These guys really know how to have a good time when the bottle is free.

I started grazing toward the front of the plane to thank my benefactors and to get out of the humidity of those sumo-sized bookends I was seated between. As I scurried to first class, I fell on an idea that could help solve my problem of nowhere to go after the policy board meetings were over on Wednesday. I couldn't afford to go to Washington early and had no money to fly home for the four days in between. I was a golfer caught in the headlights of bankruptcy.

Frank wanted to know what movie I was watching back there, and if the wine went with the French cheese that they serve in the servitude class. I told him I hope his prostate gets enlarged. After some quick bantering, I told Frank I had nothing to do from Thursday until Sunday, and since I was on the policy board making decisions about TV contracts, I should watch how a televised event is produced.

"If you could supply me with room and board, I would love to sit in the trucks and watch you do your directing thing. I could get you Cokes or coffee or whatever, your personal servant for those four days. How does that sound, Frank?"

"You're broke, aren't you?" Frank said playfully.

"No shit, Sherlock," was my dysphoric reply.

"Show up Friday for rehearsal at eleven and check into the Stouffer's on Thursday, we'll have a room for you. Now get back to the screaming kids in coach section before I have you thrown off the plane for being up here." Frank had the bedside manner of Attila the Hun sporting a bad case of hemorrhoids, but I loved him at this moment.

I showed up promptly at eleven, well fed from a gorging on room service, and weary-eyed from the menu of latest movie releases that I signed to the room. I was a pig and I enjoyed the wallow.

I opened the door to Frank's office and he bellowed from the confines of his mobile home for me to go out to the sixteenth hole. He didn't sound like he wanted to engage in light conversation, so I broke into a slight trot out toward the sixteenth. I couldn't help but wonder why I wasn't going to sit in the trucks with Frank while he was doing the telecasts, and gain some insight to how a telecast was produced, every once in a while getting Frank some snacks or casual conversation. What the hell was I going to the sixteenth hole for?

As I approached the green at the par-3 sixteenth hole, I could only assume I was going to be used as a spotter on the tee. A spotter is usually a caddie who has missed the cut and he puts on headphones and stands on the back of the tee and looks in the bag of the pros to see what club they're hitting and then relays that information to the scoring center at CBS and then it goes to the spotter in the towers, where the information is relayed to the announcer. The announcer says, "He looks like he's got a four-iron." Makes us look clairvoyant and real smart, but now you know.

As I started to walk toward the tee, a voice came serenading down from high atop the tower, beckoning me to come up. It was Verne Lundquist, the veteran announcer, who was calling. I managed my way up the tower and exchanged idle conversation with Verne and Carl, Verne's spotter. Verne then handed me a headset and told me to grab a chair. I asked what the headset was for, and he said, "Didn't Frank tell you he wanted to try you as an announcer this week?" As I weighed the decision between doing some spotting with caddies who missed the cut, or being on national television, the conversation with myself was, as usual, very short. "Where do I sit, Verne, and what do I do?"

It looks like this in the tower: there is a little enclosure surrounded with clear plastic, much like the front seat of your car, with the windshield surrounding the front and you looking out at the green. There are two monitors in front of the announcer with the picture of the action that is taking place and a current leader board. The spotter is next to you, giving you the scores and the clubs they're hitting. In this case, Carl takes up most of the room. Carl looks like he just ate a sumo wrestler; he weighs 385 pounds. There is not much room left in the front seat of this car.

My seat was outside this cubicle and next to the cameraman. It was real interesting looking down at the action for the first time. It looks incredibly easy from way up there. How can they screw up so many shots? I was above the tension, up in the clouds. My, how this view changes your perspective of the game.

My first clash with the headphones was like being in on a private conversation with Shirley MacLaine as she channeled; there were voices everywhere. The voice in my left ear was the director, Frank, and the other voices were all the announcers from their towers. Occasionally, I would get a rogue voice and I had no idea who that was. I found out later it was a guy operating a CB unit in the neighborhood who came through on our headsets. Welcome to network television.

The rehearsal went pretty smoothly. I found out two things: (1) Your conversation must be short. The action jumps all over the place and you can't get stuck in the middle of a story. (2) Never answer Frank. No one can hear Frank. Never answer anything he says directly. Those are the rules, obey at all costs.

Verne and I got along fine. He would ask me a question and I would answer as succinctly as possible, which most of the time is impossible for me. We had about thirty minutes of rehearsal and we were done. Effortless virtuosity, I thought, and I went home to have more room service and to watch those pay-per-view movies. What a great life!

The next day, my first on national television, was going

smoothly. Verne and I were clicking like a car counter on a Los Angeles freeway. He would ask a question, I would answer and then get out. I never said, "What did you say, Frank?" I was rolling.

There was a large gap between the group that had just walked off the sixteenth green and the next group that was approaching the fourteenth green, due to a starter's time that spreads the field. I had some time, so I kicked back in the chair and read some more interesting tidbits on the personal lives of the bromide golf pros.

I was awakened from my near-catatonic state by a combination of Frank throwing the action to Verne, and Verne asking me what this putt was going to do. I looked down real fast and saw nobody on the sixteenth green and the next group walking up the fifteenth fairway. What was going on?

Verne had that Nordic look of desperation as he asked me again, and Frank was starting to annoy me with "Answer him, you culturally lost dumb son-of-a-bitch golf derelict." I looked down at the green again and there still wasn't anybody around. Were they seeing ghosts or was this just a ruse to excite the poor rookie caught lost in thought? After several more verbal harassments from Frank and the look of a desperate sheepdog on the face of Verne, I decided to play along with their game. I said, "Verne, this putt should be fairly fast, because it's going down the hill toward the water." My response was met by Verne saying, "Boy you were right, Gary, that putt has gone by at least seven feet and just about on the fringe near the water." Wait a minute.

The sixteenth green at Muirfield Village golf course has no water anywhere near it, except for the drinking fountain on the tee! I made the water stuff up because the boys were trying to get the rookie and I was trying to be a smart-ass and throw them a curve. It was a wild pitch.

I heard Frank say, "Throw it to eighteen, Verne," and then he looked at me with those screeching Scandinavian eyes and asked if I could respond a little quicker next time. Frank then hit his button and began to verbally blast me for my "bradyencephalic response," which I took to mean less than congratulatory.

At this point, I realized that they weren't kidding and we were really on the air! Oh, God. "Verne, could you help me here in my moment of conjecture and look down on the sixteenth green and tell me if you see anybody, or do I have to call a ghostbuster?"

"Of course there's nobody there," said Verne. Now I really was confused. "Verne, if there's nobody there, why did you say the ball rolled seven feet by the hole when I made up the thing about the water being there in the first place?"

"There is water there," Verne said, with a stern look of what-in-the-hell-are-you-talking-about on his face.

"There's no water on this sixteenth hole," I said.

"I know that, you idiot, but we were doing the twelfth hole!"

"Wait a minute, we're doing the twelfth hole also? I was told to go out to the sixteenth hole with you."

What had happened was that, during rehearsal, we hadn't used a camera for our other hole, the twelfth, because the camera was broken. I had no way of knowing that I was also supposed to be on the twelfth hole as well as on sixteen, unless I called La Toya Jackson on the Psychic Friends hot line. Confusing business, huh?

As life weaves its reckless mysteries, the twelfth hole has water surrounding the green on this par-3. The putt had come from the top tier real fast toward the water and gone seven feet by the hole.

I had made something totally up and it just so happened to be a perfect call in this less-than-perfect business.

An idiot was born, and Frank Chirkinian has slept a total of six hours the past ten years wondering why in the world he ever took that fateful flight in the first place. Never before has the fate of so many been at the whim of one man. Enjoy your sleep, Frank. I promise to be a good boy.

The Adventures of Jacques McCord

Picture me sitting on the bottom of a pool trying to sell you on the merits of DryJoy golf shoes by Foot-Joy. They do work, because by the time I was done, the only thing that wasn't wrinkled were my feet.

If you have not seen the commercial, I, Jacques McCord, am seen looking into the camera discussing how good these shoes are in wet weather. I should know. I was gathering chlorine in my eyes, standing in the deep end of a swimming pool at Universal Studios in Orlando, Florida. I will never go swimming again.

This story started to unfold when I received a letter from the CEO of Titleist and Foot-Joy Worldwide, Wally Uihlein, wanting to know if I wanted to do another Foot-Joy commercial. The letter struck me as funny when it started out: "Gary, I can understand if you don't want to do this. Please contact me and we can discuss something else to do."

I didn't read the rest of the letter. I just went to the attachment on the letter that has the story boards. This is a picture-by-picture account of what is to be done. I'm better at pictures than I am at reading.

Let me regress for one minute. These commercials get more

airtime than those Energizer bunny commercials during Easter. Every time one is played, I get some money, and my agent gets more. They are great exposure and usually fairly harmless to shoot. It's golf. What can happen during the taping of a golf commercial?

I called my agent and inquired about the two things I hold dear to my heart: How much am I going to make and how much exposure am I going to get in this commercial? I was informed that I was going to get a great deal and I would be 90 percent of the commercial. Let's get wet, man; this should be simple.

I flew to Orlando, to Disney World. I was told I would be under two feet of water, with a capable director and divers standing by. My wake-up call at the hotel would be for 6 A.M. to be on the set by 7:30. Davis Love would be joining me for the first two hours of the shoot, and then I would continue and finish the commercial by myself.

The wake-up call was on time and I was starting to feel like Flipper. I arrived on the set, a huge pool in the back lot of Universal Studios. It was raining, and the pool was covered. I made my way to the makeup trailer and promptly went to work.

Underwater makeup takes a long time to put on. I now know what Michael Jackson goes through every morning. The one problem we were going to have was how to keep my mustache "up" during the underwater shoot. They had been working on this for a couple of days, and the makeup artist said spirit gum would keep this thing up during a meltdown at Chernobyl.

I put some acrylic long underwear on and then all the golf stuff. I was looking good, but this stuff was not drip-dry. The director and all the staff people were waiting poolside. Davis had not yet gotten there, so we went over some details.

Camera and crew were down in the water. There were

underwater speakers so the director could talk to you so you didn't have to come out of the water. They'd thought of everything.

The scene goes like this: I would be in front and mumble something about how good these shoes are when it's wet. I would then turn and ask Davis if this was right. He would mumble something underwater, and I would turn and say, "He said yes." Simple. Let's get in the pool.

I met with the diver who was going to assist me, and as we submerged into the shallow end, he asked how many dives I had made. I said, "Say what?"

"You mean you haven't had any diving experience?"

I said, "I saw *Waterworld* two times. Does that count?"

He paddled off and talked to the other divers. I was starting to feel this whole idea of me in a large water hazard wasn't going to go well. My diver, Manatee of the Deep as I called him, informed me we should work on our diving skills in the shallow end before we embarked to the cold, dark bottom. I was already starting to feel like the *Titanic*!

We worked on "buddy" breathing, as he called it, although I didn't even know the guy. He said that he would be under with me, and would supply me with the air hose so I wouldn't drown. They should call it "The-best-friend-I-have-in-life breathing system."

So Manatee of the Deep (he was bigger than one) and I practiced until we had an oxygen communication partnership. I was starting to feel comfortable.

The next thing we did was make me sink. I tried a couple of rehearsals in the water, and I started floating to the top. They wanted me secure to the bottom, so I put three lead jackets on and then taped two ten-pound weights to the insides of my knees. I now know what Ben Wright must feel like after a visit to Fat Frank's All-You-Can-Eat Barbecue. I felt swollen.

There was excitement everywhere as I made my way, with Manatee of the Deep, toward the deep end with all the camera stuff at the bottom.

"That looks deep down there, Manatee," I said. "My agent said it was only supposed to be eight feet or so of water."

"You better get a new agent, Suck Air." That was his cute name for me. "It's fifteen feet down there, and you're going to be stuck on the bottom for a while."

I sensed a strong dislike for my erstwhile agent and Manatee for the first time.

The feeling I got as I held on to Manatee with my eyes closed going to the bottom reminded me a lot of the feeling I get over a four-footer for par. Disoriented and cold.

We went down and down and down until I felt the bottom with my DryJoys. There was somebody trying to talk to me, but I couldn't hear them because of the noise the bubbles were making. I was hyperventilating like Roseanne at a doughnut shop.

The voice said, "Hi, Gary, how are you doing down there? This is the director." I got a couple of words out before I realized I could only talk to Flipper in this environment. All I could do was listen.

The director informed me that he would be talking to me as I went through lines I was going to say during the shooting of the commercial. He would say, "Remove air hose and action." I would count to three, open my eyes, find the camera, say my lines, look around to Davis Love behind me as he was saying his lines, look back to the camera and say, going out, "That means yes." Sounds easy, but so does yodeling.

To make a long story longer, I got through about half my

speech when I ran out of breath and grabbed my throat to make a choking motion. Manatee came out of the darkness with an air hose that looked like a snake breathing bubbles and stuffed it in my mouth. I gagged as I took in water, air, and some skin from his fingers. Diver's panic had set in, and I was only on my first take.

This was the first time I realized I had to rely on Manatee for air because I could not move or swim anywhere with all that weight on me. I was like Marlon Brando trying to get up out of a lawn chair.

We spent the next two hours getting the scene done so Davis could go home. Poor Davis had to stay down there while I kept screwing up. I don't think he will invite me to go snorkeling in Cancún this year.

We got that part done, and I stayed in the water for the next three hours, seven in all, to film this grisly tale from the deep. I had to stay on the bottom, fifteen feet down, with my eyes closed because of the chlorine, and could not wear a mask because it would leave a line on my face, and it would screw up my mustache. I could not venture to the top because I was overweight and Manatee was too tired taking me up and down. Right then I decided to change agents.

Here is what I learned from this experience:

Jacques Cousteau was a very brave man.

I had no fear of the water until this commercial.

I will read every letter I get offering a commercial to see what I have to do.

I will never go down in a submarine.

I will never eat a bottom fish again because I know what they go through.

I will fire my agent.

I hate the name Suck Air.

A Star Is Born

It's directed by Ron Shelton and stars Kevin Costner, Don Johnson, and Rene Russo. It's about golf; it's about life. I'm sucking oxygen, my first scene is tomorrow.

The first time I was contacted about the movie was three months ago when my agent sent me a script about this golfer who was a pretty good college player from the University of Houston. He went on to play the mini-tours and then ended up owning a driving range in the bowels of west Texas. He was a big fish in a little pond. He was surrounded by a group of life-sucking cronies that live to go to the range and vegetate their way through middle age. They could not be more happy. Roy (Tin Cup) eventually loses his driving range in a gambling debt and sets off to qualify for the U.S. Open to come up with the cash to get his life back. The process is hilarious.

Ron Shelton came to see me in Vail, Colorado, about taking a part in the movie. I asked him how much money he wanted, and Hollywood, here I come! Ron was very sincere in his conviction to make a golf movie that looked and sounded realistic.

We played golf in Vail and did some serious hiking in the Rockies, and he filled me in on what would transpire. Ron visited the Tour quite often to get a feel for the game. After reading the screenplay, I could see he was mainlining golf already, and we were in good hands.

Ron brought Kevin out to the World Series of Golf in Akron, Ohio. Kevin had just come in from Europe, where he was promoting *Waterworld*. We started on his golf game immediately. Kevin had not played that much golf before, but a better student I have never had! Watch the movie; we used no double.

The scene we are going to shoot tomorrow is one involving a charity tournament with David Sims (Don Johnson) and his caddie Tin Cup (Kevin Costner). His playing partner is Craig Stadler (Walrus) and they are playing against Phil Mickelson and myself. Peter Kostis is playing the on-course announcer.

The scene sounds simple. We drive off a par-5, then Phil and I hit the ball on the green in two. Stadler and Sims drive the ball right off the tee. Stadler goes for the green in two because Tin Cup (caddie) eggs him into doing so. Stadler hits the ball into the water and now the scene starts when Sims (Don Johnson) and Tin Cup (Kevin) get into a verbal battle about Sims wanting to lay up. Tin Cup implores him to go for it, as he would, but Sims is the third-leading money winner on the Tour, and he's going to do it his way. I have had scenes like this on the Tour. The caddie never wins!

I had been on the set for a couple of days when Stadler and Mickelson showed up at the hotel for dinner to meet the director and Kevin. Ron Shelton wanted the guys to feel comfortable with Kevin, and besides, all the wives were dying to meet him, including mine. Everyone had a ball and Ron told us that cast call would be at 6 A.M. Stadler groaned with the familiar cry of an animal caught in a rusty trap. He can't look pretty that early.

Peter Kostis picked me up at my room at six. We all had lines that we knew we would blow in front of all of Hollywood. I packed two pairs of underwear.

The next two days were shot from sunup to sundown. Twelve-hour days for a scene that will run three and a half minutes at best! I'd rather get the yips. All you do is sit and wait for the crew to set up for another angle for the camera to shoot the same take you have already done twenty times before. This will teach you patience.

There were tents on the course set up with food while you were waiting. Stadler never had so much fun! The word is he will check into the Jenny Craig clinic shortly after leaving the set. Stads was magnificent in his first role. He attacked the screen with the same panache that he attacks a driver. The rolled shoulders after a bad drive. The pounding of the driver into the bag to mark its demise. All Stadler, all good.

When you get done with the day's work, they have what they call "dailies." The film from the day is sent by plane to Hollywood, processed, and flown back for the actors and director to view at a rented movie theater for a private showing. I went to look at myself on the big screen. Thank God I have a real job.

Well, we were all sitting around talking about the last two days. Kevin was very helpful in preparing us for our close-ups. He kept telling Mickelson to smile, Stadler to pretend like he was hungry, and me not to overact. Kostis was fine, he kept whispering into the microphone. We all survived our first movie roles and will live to pass on great exaggerations until *Tin Cup* comes out. Until then, lights, camera, action! Hold it! Someone in wardrobe bring me my other pair of underwear.

Range of Dreams

I . . . HOPE this ends soon.

I just got back from the Bob Hope Classic Telethon, where we play with four different amateurs a day for four days in a row. If you are really lucky, you can get into the celebrity flight and really have some fun watching the stars unleash their borrowed swings and try to knock off the toupees of innocent bystanders who are busy unfolding their lawn chairs. It's like a movie star's shooting gallery located in Sun City.

The Hope is a very hectic week full of fun and nonsense. I started by emceeing the shoot-out on Tuesday between ten of the top money winners on the PGA Tour where the format is a per-hole elimination until there are only two players left coming down the eighteenth hole. My job is to cause chaos and insurrection amongst the players until they have no conscious thought left. I have been told I do it well.

Because this tournament is a five-day event over four different golf courses, you are very limited with your practice rounds. The idea is just to get ready for very slow play and some of the worst-looking plaid outfits that ever came out of the Eisenhower era.

The pros go to play nine holes at a couple of the golf courses to see how the greens and roughs are and get an idea of the different grasses. You don't want to beat yourself up trying to play all of the golf courses, because this is a long week early in the year. The Hope is a survival test of putting up with cameras going off while celebrities dote over their fans during the middle of your backswing. You actually get used to it. I am told it will make me a better person.

This year I had the privilege of playing with Kevin Costner, John Elway, Matt Williams, Leslie Nielsen, Derrick Thomas, the great linebacker for the Kansas City Chiefs, and Andy Williams. We had lots of laughs when I was making birdies and no fun at all when I was making bogeys. We were crying more than we were laughing, but that's the nature of this game.

My real job was to chaperon Kevin Costner around for the week, day and night. Tough job, right, ladies? I had been with Kevin for the last three and a half months on the set of the movie *Tin Cup*. Kevin has not been around golf long, so I wanted to make his first venture into our world of professional golf a fun and wonderful experience. It also got me some free meals at night.

I might now tell you about Kevin's golf game. He came to me about two weeks before we started shooting the movie to work on his golf swing. One of my jobs was to make him look like he could win the U.S. Open while millions of people would be going to movie theaters trying to find the action shots where we used a double to trick them. We used no double in any of the golf sequences. It was all Kevin.

The golf swing is very hard to fake, and I'm willing to bet no other actor could have pulled this off. It was an amazing performance. He is without a doubt the quickest study I have ever had. My friend Peter Kostis and I worked with him the first day on developing a swing that would look good in front of the cameras. We changed literally everything he had done before, and he stuck to it like makeup sticks to Tammy Faye Bakker.

We played the first day together, and off the tenth at Bermuda Dunes, our first hole, I have never been more nervous, but it was for Kevin.

The hardest thing he had to learn was how to tee the ball up. Really! The first time I saw him tee it up, he looked like a club-footed carpenter trying to hammer a nail in the floor with Rollerblades on—you get the picture. So I wandered over close to the tee marker just in case he had trouble teeing the ball up.

As he approached the ball, I thought, What if this poor guy whiffs it in front of all these people? He'll never play the game again and I won't get a ride in his Gulfstream G-3 airplane. What thoughts were racing through my mind as he took his customary waggle, pulled at his shirtsleeve, and took a glance down the fairway?

He started the club back slow; I started to get a sickening feeling in the pit of my lower intestine. The rhythm was good, the change of direction was flawless, and the ball went straight down the middle with a hint of a hook. My God, he did it! Needless to say, I was all smiles, and as Kevin leaned over to pick up the tee, he gave me a sly wink to say, "I fooled 'em for one shot!"

I have heard of actors and their huge egos. Hell, in any business in which you are successful, you are entitled to have an ego. The motion picture business has its share of these senseless sponges of mock adoration, but I'm willing to bet that if I put you in Kevin Costner's shoes, you wouldn't have gone through with this exercise in self-degradation. Here is a guy who has barely started playing this difficult game, who goes out in front of thousands of people at the golf course and millions of people on national TV and exposes every little flaw in his tender game. What it also exposed was the higher platform that his character resides on. He did not have to go out and humiliate himself; instead, he put his ego aside and showed those people he can play this game of golf.

They didn't care, they wanted to see the guy who played in *Bull Durham*, *Field of Dreams*, *The Bodyguard*, *Dances with Wolves*, *Waterworld*. What they saw was a guy named Roy McAvoy from Salome, Texas, who owns his own driving range and aspires to make it big on the PGA Tour. *Tin Cup* is a movie about an encounter between character and circumstance, and Kevin Costner has a lot of character.

Celebrity Hacks

Over the years, celebrity golf has ravaged our land. You can't go to a Tour event and not see the latest new artist from the country-music station swinging his Elvis-like lower body through the hitting area. Guitar on his shoulder, and melancholy on his lips, he rides the tournament trail, singing and swinging into the sunset.

The athletic wonders of the world have picked up the game to suffice their craving for competition after the sweaty world of labor disputes and megalomaniacal owners have let the air out of their ball. They pursue golf with the same fervor they put into their jockstraps for the big game. After they retire, they shoot big game or play golf on the celebrity golf circuit.

Athletes have replaced the actors for print recognition on the links. If you want to have a successful golf tournament, just have Michael Jordan show up; double your profits and double your security!

Rockers have made inroads to the banal bastion of country club golf. Rock 'n' roll by night, rock and sway on the golf course by day. Golf is basically their downer after grueling road shows at night. They go to the quiet confine of a country club and enjoy the scenery and serenity of the polyester civilization. This is their drug rehab. No need to go see Betty if you're watching a half-topped five-wood head for a duck trying to mate in the pond guarding the front of the green on the ninth hole. Just go to your bag, grab some more free balls you have extorted from Titleist, and bang away! Just like your lead guitarist.

Old presidents are a staple at any professional golf tourney held in Palm Springs. That's where they hang out between speaking engagements and gubernatorial balls. The warm climate mixes well with their Republican platforms. If you can get a blend of rockers, retired athletes, and old Republican presidents, you can have one helluva eclectic gallery. They'll have tattoos, be wearing new glow-in-the-night Nikes, and have lawn chairs draped over their leather tanned arms, trying to comb their blue hair with their senior citizens' discount card. It's a sight the tour caddies talk about for months.

Movie stars, movie stars. These are the people galleries flock to see. The grace and movement of a Bob Hope drive, the uncanny putting stroke of Clint Eastwood, and the steely determination of Jack Lemmon bearing down on a seven-footer for an eight. Goose bumps go up and down my support hose.

Bing Crosby started this cavalcade of movie stars and the marriage to golf in 1937. At the Rancho Santa Golf Club near San Diego, California, he held a one-day tournament won by Sam Snead. Bing invited some of his backstage buddies to hang around with the professional golfers, and the clambake began. They would remain there until 1941 and then move to the Monterey Peninsula. The Crosby had a home, and it had some of the wildest parties this side of a housewarming at Caligula's.

General Dwight D. Eisenhower, the most famous golfing president; Arnold Palmer, the pirate in polyester; and television in the late fifties and early sixties exploded golf into the sports scene. This was the lethal combination that let golf squeeze into the venue of big-time sports.

I have had the opportunity to play the Tour for the last three decades. I have hunted the wayward golf ball in many streams and ecologically sensitive areas inhabited by hunter-gatherer celebrities. Believe me, they hunt with the same ferocity for their ball as we do. Losing a ball is a very debilitating ritual in our society for peasant or royalty.

This is what I remember.

If we get to the back nine, I'll need a cart group:

BOB HOPE—I first played with Bob Hope back in the eighties at the Jerry Ford Invitational. I believe it was '88 and that's how old Bob was at the time. He had a very smooth swing that he probably developed doing all those road shows with Bing Crosby.

Mr. Hope would play constantly to the galleries on the first and last holes. During the round he would grind hard on his score, usually trying to beat President Ford in a little money game. When I rode in the cart with him, he would rattle off joke after joke. He was very sharp at eighty-eight!

In the mid-nineties he was losing the warranty on his mind and didn't play much golf, other than a ceremonial swing off the first tee. The Tour owes a lot to this man, who had a tournament with his name that has been part of the PGA Tour since 1965.

PRESIDENT FORD—Has assaulted more people with a golf club than Jack Nicholson. Who can remember those days at the Bob Hope

Classic when President Ford would tee off on the first hole and send a Scud into the gallery and some lucky senior citizen would be marked ceremonially by the imprint of his golf ball? During one tournament, I witnessed the entire galley showing up wearing hard hats on the first tee. They were probably all Democrats.

President Ford worked on his game with the passion of an incumbent Republican up for reelection. His game is very respectable. We are both members at Country Club of the Rockies in Vail, Colorado, and I get to see quite a bit of the President. To this day, he still asks the membership chairman how in the world McCord could belong to a club of which *he* is a member. President Ford still doesn't remember his adopting me in 1974.

JACK LEMMON—My lasting memory of Jack Lemmon will be in that crouched putting stance, eyes narrowly focused, poised over a six-foot putt on the seventeenth hole at Pebble Beach, shaking like a Mexican space shuttle, for an eight. Attired handsomely in an ensemble of canary yellow shirt and sweater draped lavishly over spoiled banana yellow pants that reek of polyester. He and his professional partner, Peter Jacobsen, would be seventeen shots out of the cut, but Jack would be trying harder than a hooker during shore leave to make that putt for an eight. Jack Lemmon is a grinder.

A nicer man you could not meet. Always congenial and ready to sign an autograph. Put him on the golf course and he has the demeanor of a man who has kidney stones and both shoes are too tight. He is focused and fragile.

Jack's Holy Grail is to make the cut at the AT&T Pebble Beach National Pro-Am. Life would stop and Jack would get off if he accomplished this seemingly impossible feat. How impossible? Jack's loyal partner, Peter Jacobsen, won the tournament in 1995 and they still missed the cut!

GEORGE C. SCOTT—I played with George in the late seventies at the Bing Crosby at Pebble Beach, as it was called then and forever more. He had sailed his boat from Los Angeles and crashed it in a violent storm. He was very sore and had bruises all over. I don't remember how he played, he wasn't that keen on the game. In fact I don't remember ever seeing him again at another tournament. I hope I had nothing to do with it.

The one thing I do remember is how scared I was of him. I remember seeing the movie *Patton*, and I kept thinking he would shoot me with those pearl-handled guns if I ever screwed up a shot. The tournament went without incident.

CLINT EASTWOOD—"Dirty Harry" is the quietest guy you could ever be around. Has that certain Hollywood cool you see in the movies. His golf game lacks the power and grace that this big man can generate. A converted tennis player, he hits the ball like he's performing a drop shot. Underneath it, and it doesn't go very far. I can't believe I'm saying that about Detective Callahan!

If he had had some good instruction a few years ago, Clint could have been a decent player. I really don't think he gives a damn about the game, Clint just plays it to be sociable with his friends.

One thing for sure, if he reads this, I won't get any free rooms at his Mission Ranch in Carmel, and I'll probably get roughed up the next time I walk into the Hogs Breath, his local watering hole. Glass Chin McCord is what they call me.

VIC DAMONE—Vic's golf swing has the same flow as one of his soft ballads, but has the power of Pee-Wee Herman. Beautiful to watch, but the club doesn't make enough noise on the downswing. Vic is forever taking lessons from Mac O'Grady and has improved his vocabulary considerably. Mac and Vic are dear friends and spend countless hours on the practice range at Thunderbird.

Vic Damone is one of the grandest guys you could hang with. When I get back to Palm Springs, I'll just have to go over to Thunderbird and see what Mac and Vic are working on next.

JAMES GARNER—Jim is one of the best-ever movie stars to play this game. In his younger years he could play to a four handicap, and that was not an ego handicap that fills the plate of some of Tinsel Town's proneurs.

Jim handles himself on the golf course with all the class he maintains on the big screen. Football and movie stunts have been hard on his knees and he can't play the game like he could. We rarely see "Rockford" anymore on the celebrity swing of the PGA Tour, but I see him in reruns all the time.

There's a madman inside of me and he's hacking away.

Rockers who have mutated to this game:

ALICE COOPER—The first time I played golf with Alice Cooper, in the VH1 Fairway to Heaven Tournament, he had a long putt on the second hole and left it considerably short. I couldn't help myself: "Nice putt, Alice" was my obvious reply. "I've never heard that one before," said the demonic rocker.

Alice Cooper, snakes hanging all over him, singing of mayhem and twisted bodies, is a nine-handicapper who loves golf and is devoted to his family and his church. Who would of thunk it!

Alice is a very good player. Hits it fairly long off the tee and has a nice command of all of his shots. One thing's for sure, I will never follow him into the bushes to find a ball. He still scares the hell out of me.

HOOTIE AND THE BLOWFISH—Also met these guys at the VH1 Fairway to Heaven Tournament in 1994. Mark Bryan, the lead guitarist, asked *me* for my autograph. I obliged and asked him what group he was with. "Hootie and the Blowfish" was the unexpected reply. "We watch you on TV every chance we get. We love the game" was Mark's answer. I started looking around for a TV camera, figuring someone is busting my balls. No TV camera around anywhere. Mark brought the rest of the guys over and introduced me, Soni, Dean, and Darius. We exchanged small talk and off I went to the bar. I saw Craig Stadler standing there and asked him if he had ever heard of a group called Heidi and the Glowworms. Stads said, "Have another drink." I did.

After their CD *Cracked Rear View* was released, everyone, including me, knew it was Hootie and the Blowfish! We kept in touch and they persuaded me to help them get into anything that involved golf. They were nuts about the game and still are.

They would appear at Tour events and hang around in the TV tower with me. Darius wants to be a sports announcer. Now he's just getting rich.

I've only known Hootie for three years, but they have not changed since that day we first met in Orlando. Fame has not soured the Fish.

All of their golf games semi-suck, but they have a ball playing the game. They promised to come see Peter Kostis and myself down at Grayhawk in Scottsdale, Arizona, after this last concert tour is over and we'll work on their swings. Peter and I will probably just take the "semi" out of the "suck."

VINCE GILL—Well, he's not a rocker, but he did start out as one! This country-and-western soprano is a golf sampler plate. He plays every waking moment of his hillbilly life. He is the best golfer, by far, of the tattooed set.

Vince sports a two handicap and polishes it frequently on road trips. He can "twang" that thing off the tee with most of us on the Tour and has a pretty good short game. Vince's only bad note is that sometimes he ignites into hyperspace on the course. A cold shower and a picture of Roseanne naked couldn't cool him off!

Vince has his own golf tournament in Nashville, Tennessee, and many of the local charities benefit from his love of the game.

MIKE MILLS—R.E.M. never thought they would have someone in their group with the best golf swing of any of the rockers. Mike has played golf for many years and has a swing that should be on a motivational video. He also plays as much as he can while on that "road to nowhere."

RICHIE SAMBORA (BON JOVI)—Just starting to play the game. Hopefully, he'll bring along his wife, Heather Locklear. I would not charge her for lessons.

EDDIE VAN HALEN—Also just starting to play the game. Hopefully, he'll bring along his wife, Valerie Bertinelli. I would not charge her for lessons either.

BRUCE HORNSBY—In a song from the CD of the movie *Tin Cup*, Bruce says, "I got me a big stick and I'm swinging in the dirt." Bruce needs a big stick; he's 6′5″ tall. Doesn't play much golf while he's touring, but gets out once in a while to "enjoy the outdoors, and think of a new song."

Guys who like to switch the size of the balls they play with.

Jocks who have an itch for the game:

JOHNNY BENCH—"Squat" has the biggest hands I have ever seen on a white man. That is probably the reason he never became a gynecologist.

J.B. has a passion for the game. He has been well tutored by Mac O'Grady and myself and can still talk without stuttering. He has a fine swing that produces plenty of club head speed. What would one expect from a pull hitter!

The only soft spot in his game is that his putter has the "take" sign on all the time. He never produced much with it.

CHARLES BARKLEY—If you compared his golf game to basketball, he probably would be a 30 percent shooter from the floor, and with his putter he would be like Shaq from the foul line. But does he love to play! He and Michael have played for more money on the back nine than I have made in my career. Hundreds have been exchanged.

Now that he has been traded to Houston, I'll miss seeing him at Grayhawk. I won't go to many more Suns games either!

MICHAEL JORDAN—Has an out-and-out addiction to the game. Would play at night if his wife would let him. Has probably helped our sport gain more in popularity than he will ever know. Minorities will gravitate to this game now, more than ever, since his "airness" has made it cool.

I have played with Michael a couple of times and have enjoyed his company. I remember walking to the first tee at Desert Mountain, in Scottsdale, and telling Michael I couldn't afford to play him for enough to get his heart started. He told me I was right and we played for $100 units and I gave him eight strokes. I don't think my win affected his cash flow.

I hope Michael continues to enjoy this game. His presence has helped lift golf to new corners of our social map.

The new blood off the movie set.

New box office hits:

JACK NICHOLSON, SLY STALLONE, AND ARNOLD SCHWARZENEGGER—All new to the game, but won't bring it out on the Tour for ridicule. If you just come on out and play, we promise to give you two thumbs up!

JOE PESCI—Now, this guy is more fun than going out with Hugh Grant! Joe is in constant motion on the golf course. Telling you what kind of shot he's going to play. Telling the wife of the club president she ought to have that wart removed from her chin. Talking to the squirrels and telling them they're all nuts. This guy has some serious gravity.

Joe's golf swing has more positions than a Craftmatic adjustable bed. But he can play. He's got that New Jersey bravado, or street savvy, that can get him through any occasion. He is one of my favorite celebrities to hang around and I pay him considerably to do so.

JAMES WOODS—One of the great character actors of our time has the shortest swing you will ever see. It looks like he got his swing at a half-off sale. Needs to increase the length of his swing so he can put some "whoop" on the ball and enjoy the par-5s more. Played in his first AT&T in '96.

DON JOHNSON—The smarmy character David Sims in *Tin Cup* is a pretty good golfer. Don played the adversary of Kevin Costner in this movie and had many golf swing scenes. His swing doesn't have enough width going back and coming through to look like a Tour player's swing. So in the movie scenes we would put a plastic ball down for him to hit, or no ball at all, and he duplicated what we wanted perfectly. Like everyone else, if we put a real golf ball down for him to hit, he would resort to his old swing. Another take, please.

Don has a pretty good idea what to do on the golf course and plays as much as he can between shootings of his new show, *Nash Bridges*.

CHEECH MARIN—Plays the sidekick of Don in his new series and got the job when they worked together on the set of *Tin Cup*. Cheech didn't play golf at all when the movie started, but with the help of my Tour caddie, Steve Lewison, he could actually hit the ball down the fairway with some sort of decorum. Cheech and his son would run to the course after every scene was done and play until it got dark. I hope he continues to play the game, he is one funny son of a bitch.

KEVIN COSTNER—Again, the lasting impression I will have of Kevin Costner is how fast he learned the mechanics of the swing. He had only played golf once a year with his father-in-law, and then to go out on the PGA Tour and play in the pro-ams a short three months later is testament to his athletic ability and his character.

The last thing you would expect a Hollywood superstar to do is show any weaknesses to the admiring public. But Kevin braved the frigid waters of a golf novice and delighted fans with his play and his smile.

Kevin has a tendency to get a little frustrated with himself at times on the golf course. I keep telling him he hasn't spilled enough of his soul to the game to bark at its frustrations.

He likes the game now, he doesn't love it. It's just a little too slow for him. Kevin will play as many pro-ams as his schedule will allow and for that, all the ladies will be very happy!

BILL MURRAY—The axis of this guy's world is a little tipped. The only celebrity golfer in the world I would *pay* to watch play golf. This guy is fully calibrated for fun.

One of the times we played together was at the Kapalua Invitational in Maui, Hawaii. The wind was blowing toupees all over the place and Bill was late to the tee. He finally came striding up the tee in black golf shoes, purple calf socks, overalls that were cut off as shorts, and a Hawaiian shirt that had cigars stuffed into the pocket. He was wearing one of those Chinese "coolie" hats which had a brim the size of Nova Scotia. He told me he was playing a Titleist 3, no cut, and let's rock.

Playing the ninth hole I heard a commotion to the right of where Bill had driven his ball near a pineapple field. A crowd had gathered around and laughter was in the air. I knew Bill must be up to something, so I walked over to take a look. He had found this elderly Hawaiian woman, distinctly dressed in native wear and defiantly secure in her heritage. Bill had pulled out of the ground some large stalks of grass, maybe three feet in length, and was stuffing them down her skirt so the grass was flowing over her lower attire. He grabbed his Big Bertha driver and started to play it like a ukulele, exhorting the native Hawaiian, "Hula, hula, till you can't hula no more." She took off her shoes and danced while Bill was strumming his forty-three-inch, stiff-shafted ukulele. Mel Brooks couldn't have done this scene better! I paused, and thought how insignificant my three-wood lay-up shot was at this moment. Bill can define moments.

Bill has a golf swing you could take to show-and-tell. Great mechanics, and his short game is getting shiny under the tutelage of the short game Obi Wan, Dave Pelz. He looks much better than his eighteen handicap would indicate.

The total package of Bill Murray is a Salvador Dalí print. Bill, standing in front of you, looks like the victim of a hate crime. If Charles Darwin had studied him first, I wonder if he would have come up with the same conclusions on evolution. Bill's attire provokes images of mass immigrant migrations. He is adrift on the sartorial seas. His antics on the golf course are genius in concept and side-splittingly funny to watch. I truly believe he is the victim of an alien abduction and they sent him back early because he was causing havoc in the spacecraft. Welcome back to earth. I love Bill Murray.

Taking the Bite Out of Ben

There had to exist a place, a long, long time ago, in the bowels of a quaint English village where a fairy tale of gruesome proportions took place. That would have been the upbringing of Ben Wright, the swine who has offended my character over and over again on CBS golf telecasts. He is the main reason I don't sleep at night.

Ben Wright has been doing golf on CBS for the past twenty-two years. An open wound is he. Ben was a writer for the *London Financial Times* and still does some writing when they are in desperate need. He got the job when a brilliant English journalist turned golf commentator named Henry Longhurst died and left a foreign voice void in CBS's golf coverage. The rest is anticlimactic.

I am fond of Ben Wright, like I am fond of a head cold. We have been working together for the last seven years and he has improved my vocabulary quite a bit. His verbal tongue-lashings on the air about my illiteracy have made me a better person.

I will now embark on a true story about Ben Wright. He cannot deny it. Nor will he.

During the Western Open of 1978, on a Saturday night, Ben

Wright was looming over the commode in his plush suite, armed with a bad cough. Trying to the best of his abilities to relieve himself and not hit his shoe.

Coughing throughout this demonstration proved costly. As he reached down to flush the commode, one last cough dislodged his upper bridge and he helplessly watched it swirl down the toilet.

A baptism of his false teeth he didn't need at this time. We engage in a ritual of boring proportions every Saturday and Sunday morning during which we don our best food-stained ties and go to the eighteenth tower to do "Hole Openings." These simply provide the viewer with a fact on each particular hole, as we explain, with morbid fascination, the complexities of our holes.

When Ben tried to talk, he sounded like Gabby Hayes auditioning for a part in *My Fair Lady*. In my opinion, he never sounded better.

In a very desperate measure, Ben called the night janitor and explained the situation in his best King's English, sans his upper bridge. Once the communication gap was broken, off they went into the hotel's sewer deposit, located in the basement, armed with sanitary gloves and a gallon of Listerine, just in case they found his teeth. Their expectations were high, but their efforts were futile.

Dawn was approaching, and so was the upcoming on-camera hole introduction. At this point, the bridge-free Ben Wright lay down for some rest and plotted his walk through the yellow pages to see if he could find a dentist open on Sunday morning. The toothless swine never slept better.

As 9 A.M. approached, a dentist was found and alerted to his problem. Time was of the essence, and the dentist obliged.

Ben knocked on the door of his office at 9:20, and as the dentist appeared, Ben, with great difficulty, and sounding as if he was speaking through an invisible kazoo, said, "I need sssssome teeeeeth." Dr. Charlie Fu responded with, "What seems to be the problem, Mr. Light?" Sherlock Holmes meets Charlie Chan. What an office visit!

With great speed and little concern for craftsmanship, time was of the essence, Dr. Fu fitted Ben with some dentures that looked like they would fit Carol Channing. But it was done.

Off to the golf course he rushed, going over his upcoming hole introduction with persistence.

Word had gotten out in the CBS compound and they were ready.

Ben made his way through the exercise with great agility and great secrecy. No one had noticed his new choppers! Or so he thought.

But as the tournament came on live and everybody across the nation watched Ben's hole introduction take place, with Ben's voice describing the serene seventeenth hole, and his adorable cartoon face gone, the director substituted a pair of dimestore clacking teeth that walked across the screen, with Ben's melodious tones inspiring their every clank.

He is the bane of my existence, and I must go on. I will fight his evil existence until I win a tournament. In other words, I'm in for a long fight.

Frank

It must have been like studying at the feet of Pablo Picasso, the charging bull of modern art. Maybe it was like being a cast member at the Globe Theater when Shakespeare's troupe was performing *The Taming of the Shrew*. The piano, maybe, of Wolfgang Amadeus Mozart, as he lifted his genius to a new level pounding on those keys.

I, too, have had the pleasure of working under a true genius who formulated the way our industry treats golf on television. Sure, golf doesn't have the romanticism of art or literature, but golf is what I do, and I have had the opportunity to work under the man who invented the way this game is brought to you in your living room. I am deeply affected by everything he taught me.

Frank Chirkinian started working for CBS on September 10, 1950. The network has been deeply influenced by his presence ever since. He directed different venues of sport, but settled in on golf because, as Frank says, "there are no parameters in golf, you create form live." Frank's first golf telecast was the 1958 PGA Championship in luminous black and white. He showed the last three holes, and televised golf was culturally captured.

The Masters was first viewed in 1959 and Frank was at the

helm, as he is today, thirty-seven years later. Frank became such an integral part of the tournament, he chose to become a part of the community as well. He still resides there. From his early acquaintance with the tournament's founder, Bobby Jones, he formulated the philosophy that he goes by today in presenting this sport to the viewing golf junkie. Bobby Jones told Frank that all people were interested in seeing were golf shots, plenty of golf shots. Frank's idea of rapid-fire switching from player to player was impregnated by those early conversations with Bobby Jones.

The innovations that this man is responsible for in televised golf are extraordinary. He was the one who used the blimp for the first time to show overhead views of the golf course. The blimp brought a larger view of the playing area and Frank's canvas grew accordingly.

Frank was the one who chose to use handheld cameras on the ground to get a closer viewpoint of the action. The hard camera settings on the towers were previously the only pictures provided, and distanced the action severely. In one case, during the 1960 PGA Championship at Firestone Country Club in Akron, Ohio, Frank didn't have enough cameras and needed one for the back of the eighteenth tee. He had the technicians put a large mirror behind the tee and reflected the image off the mirror from the camera on the seventeenth hole and then reversed the image. Everything worked great until the wind started blowing. Everybody looked like they were doing the hula as the mirror shook violently. Frank was not afraid to improvise and no one at CBS questioned him in those days.

The scoring system was also something with which he tinkered. In the old days, the scores as they were posted were cumulative. If the camera showed Arnold Palmer on the leader board on the sixty-eighth hole of the tournament, his score of four under par would read 261. It was an ongoing work of labor. Frank changed that to read −4, and scoreboards were forever viewer-friendly.

He put boom mikes on the course so the effects could be heard of a tee shot hit by Jack Nicklaus and the like; then in the CBS match play championship he put mikes on the players and you could finally hear what was going on between the players and their caddies as they focused on the shot ahead. The three-second-delay switch was imperative in those days!

As the cameras looked vainly for the holes, the viewing audience strained as well. Frank decided the viewer needed some help as the golf balls approached the hole, so he had the inside of the tops of the holes painted white so you could see them more clearly. Everything was done with the viewer in mind.

Frank had an influence with some of the top names in broadcasting in his thirty-seven years with CBS. He has directed the likes of: Jim McKay, Jack Whitaker, Pat Summerall, Vin Scully, Ben Wright, Ken Venturi, Jimmy Demaret, Byron Nelson, Dave Marr, John Derr, Ray Scott, Chris Schenkel, Bud Palmer, Henry Longhurst, Jim Nantz, and countless others who have benefited from his knowledge of the sport. Frank would say, "Remember, brevity, my dear boys, let the pictures tell the story, not your words."

Frank's first day with the legendary Henry Longhurst was at Pleasant Valley Country Club in Sutton, Massachusetts. It was raining hard and play was suspended. Henry called Frank from his tower on sixteen, which was next to the clubhouse, and asked Frank, "Can I go to the clubhouse and get equally as wet on the inside as I am on the outside?" "Yes, you may," Frank said, and Henry scurried down from the tower and got an adult beverage in the clubhouse. When Henry came back on the air, he was quite talkative and Frank told him his words were getting in the way of the pictures and to quit doing a radio version of the television broadcast. Henry was used to doing six to seven hours on the BBC in England for golf and did nothing but talk incessantly. American television was different, as Frank had invented it! You let the pictures do the talking. Longhurst said, "Frank, I will eliminate the persiflage." With his newfound concise banter, Henry became a legend in the industry. Just another Frank Chirkinian creation.

As Frank Chirkinian winds down his unparalleled career and the powers that be release him from what he so loves to do, I am able to reflect on what he has passed on to me in this business of showing golf on network television. He was a developer of talent. He molded their attack on the tube. He once told me, "You can bend their egos, but don't bruise them." Let the announcers do what they do best, but direct the hell out of them because we're basically idiots.

In my particular case, Frank was talking to Jim Nantz, the network's voice. Jim and I were sitting in a golf cart about ready to depart to our assignment on the sixteenth hole. It was Jim's first telecast with CBS, and Frank Chirkinian wanted Jim to know what was expected of him. After a lengthy lecture, Frank was done and Jim sped off to his assigned hole full of directions. I had been working for three short weeks and Frank had never said anything to me. I asked Frank what my responsibilities were. He stopped, glared back at me, and said, "I'll let you know when you fuck up." Frank, with that very short description, had defined my curriculum at CBS. Try anything I wanted and he'd let me know if I'd gone too far. I have tried many bizarre things during telecasts; some he has let me get away with and others he has chopped off my head for trying. A headless announcer is the best kind, as Frank might say!

For as long as I am involved with television, and life, Frank Chirkinian's teachings will be close to me. He taught me about this business like no one ever could. I feel very privileged to have walked near his shadow. There is a sense in which no gift is ours 'til we have thanked the giver.

Frank is walking toward the final curtain of his illustrious career at CBS. This golf thing has been his morphine. His new fix will come with life after golf. Whatever he decides to do, I know one thing: he will direct the hell out of it!

Thanks, Frank.

Spike Marks

High Jinks on the Diamond

I'm going to tell you a story that is true. It has nothing to do with golf, but it started on a golf course. Besides, it's my book and I'll write what I want. It was back in 1978 when I was living near San Diego. The L.A. Dodgers were coming to town. Tommy John and Don Sutton called wanting to know if I wished to play golf that afternoon before a night game. I had known Tommy and Don well from playing golf, and had worked out with the Dodgers in Vero Beach on a couple of occasions. I had a 67-mph fastball and didn't like showering with other men, however, so the major leagues were out of the question.

I showed up at Carlton Oaks Country Club right on time, thirty minutes late. It was a wonderful Friday afternoon and I knew full well I was going to coax these boys out of their per diem. The air was ripe with optimism.

Andy Messersmith, Tommy John, Don Sutton, and I teed off, sarcastic comments out of the way and love in the air. We breezed through the front side, stopping just long enough at the halfway house for some more beer and friendly presses. Then to the back side for some more bonding. You know, baseball players scratch their nuts when they're playing golf, too. Must be an outdoors thing.

Andy was drifting through his second six-pack of Bud when I turned left in the cart and he went right. It looked like a split-fingered fastball as he went down and away. I thought the boys in the other cart were going to run over him as they followed behind, but a sudden stop avoided a mishap, and Sutton handed Andy another beer as he was lying in the semi-rough on this tough par-4. What sportsmanship!

The rest of the day went without occasion, and toward the end of the round they wanted to know if I was coming to tonight's game. I told them I was going with a bunch of my buddies from our golf group called "the Thumpers," and we would be in a private box above left field. It's a great country.

I regaled them with stories about the trips this band of felons would make to sporting events, and the gambling that went on. Andy burped, apologized, and then wanted to know if they could help in hedging some bets that I might want to make during the course of tonight's game. Not a bad idea, I thought. "You mean, you could get the guys to perform certain preplanned activities during the course of the game?" I asked with a hand on my wallet. Don Sutton then told me, "Come down to the field while we're warming up and we'll ask Lasorda if that's possible." High jinks on the diamond, I was getting wet with anticipation.

I drove to the game early, with the excuse to the Thumpers that I needed to get a price on a "tuck and roll" job in nearby Tijuana, Mexico. The dumb bastards bought it. What did you expect from sociably senile underachievers, doctorates from MIT? I arrived about an hour and a half before the game and talked my way down to field level where I could get the attention of Sutton, Messersmith, or John. Don Sutton came to my rescue and was shortly joined by Tommy John. Andy was nursing a hangover in the whirlpool. None of these starters was scheduled to work, and boredom has its insanity.

They quickly called Tommy Lasorda over. He had linguini all over his face and a bib over his collar covering his Dodger blue. Tommy cannot state a sentence without colorful language. I encountered a rainbow of conversation and the proposition was put to him. "You mean you want these assholes to take fucking dives out on the motherfucking diamond while we're in a motherfucking pennant fucking race?"

"Fuckin' A," I responded.

"That sounds like fun. T.J., take down what he wants to do and we'll handle it. Now, my linguini is getting fucking cold and I'm getting tired of talking to your pansy golfing ass. See you at the World Series!" Tommy waddled back to his pasta and we made plans for the upcoming chicanery.

Of the three perpetrators, Andy was still in the whirlpool working on his "head cold"; Don, Tommy, and I were crouched in the dugout drawing up the battle plan. Five different "experiments" during the course of a nine-inning game at specific times. "Can we be arrested for doing this?" I asked nobody in particular. "Probably, but this would be our first offense, and besides, Lasorda needs us for the pennant race. They'll never lock us up," chuckled Sutton. Off I went to the private box where the pigeons were beginning to nest.

They were all there, thirty-two fun-loving Thumper Padre lovers who were wearing some sort of ugly mustard brown shirt that symbolized the Padre team colors. They looked collectively like a landslide that had come down from a Tijuana suburb. But they were a gaming bunch.

I was perched up near the top of the box with the leader of the Thumpers, Mad Dog Skuba. The Dodgers took the field for warm-ups. Mad Dog knew of the ruse. I was getting chills up and down my cheating spine and geared my pen for the upcoming bets.

The Dodger outfielders would run from the third-base foul line out to center field and back again to loosen up. The bet called for Rick Monday to trip and fall in center field on the fourth sprint. The national anthem was about to be sung and the home crowd was poised for a win.

"Okay, boys, let's get the fun machine started. I'll bet you a Dodger trips and falls in centerfold, right on his face. Give me a ten-to-one on that miracle." Mad Dog readied the pad as the bets and comments flowed. Twenty out of the thirty-two derelicts took the action and the other twelve were locking horns in a dice game that had broken out in the corner. They were supposed to check into Gamblers Anonymous the next day.

As twenty pairs of eyes focused on the six Dodgers running their wind sprints, there was a sudden hush as Rick Monday started his Chevy Chase impersonation in centerfold. Rumblin', stumblin', bumblin', he made the worst pratfall ever and slid into a headfirst fall in the bowels of centerfold. Bet won.

There were many stinging comments toward myself, as Mad Dog dutifully wrote the names of all the losers. My strategy was to lose, politely, between the setups we had planned. "You can't win 'em all, not even these guys are that stupid," offered Mad Dog.

Here are some of the bets made between the sure things we had arranged:

1. Morganna would come on the field and give Lasorda the Heimlich maneuver. 100-to-1
2. Steve Yeager, the Dodger catcher, would catch the entire second inning without his chest protector. 75-to-1

3. The San Diego Chicken would get plucked by Lasorda, then roasted and eaten during the seventh-inning stretch. 2-to-1
4. California would secede from the Union. 50-to-1 (only Confederates could take this one)
5. The next pitch would be hit for a home run by the home team and the fans would throw it back. 20-to-1
6. Within ten minutes, nobody could find a concessioner that could speak English. 300-to-1
7. Steve Garvey would impregnate someone during the course of the game. 3-to-1
8. There would be a rainout. 25-to-1 (hasn't been one in San Diego in history). I got two takers on this. Both Sioux Indians, we don't exclude anyone from being a Thumper.
9. I would win a major golf tournament in the upcoming year. 10,000-to-1. Everybody took this action.
10. The umpire would call "illegal formation" on Rollie Fingers's mustache during the ninth inning. 35-to-1. One guy took it, Dan Fouts in the skybox next to us.

So with bets like these, laced in between the sure things, I couldn't be found out. Most of these guys had the intellect of cheese. My scam was working.

The second inning called for a Dodger to "lose his cap and fall to the ground while play was going on," 5-to-1. There was a hard smash to right field and the right fielder raced and dove, what a catch! In the melee, his hat came off and hit the ground. I jumped up with enthusiasm and acknowledged my good luck. Little did they know that the left fielder, Dusty Baker, was supposed to lose his hat. I had an ace in the hole. After the second out, I told all who would listen I'd be willing to bet 25-to-1 that another hat hits the ground with only one out to go. Everybody jumped on this one.

After two foul tips at the plate, I was getting restless. I grabbed the binoculars and looked to the dugout to see what was going on, and why Dusty hadn't dusted his hat. There was Don Sutton standing on the steps yelling out to left field, "Dusty, lose the hat, now!" With a sudden flick of the wrist, the hat came off on the warning track. I jumped up again, just about pulling a groin. "My God, it's happened again!" The boys were now starting to wonder.

During the seventh, a Dodger's shoe was to come off his foot while they were on field. 20-to-1. The boys were getting betting weary. The dice game had broken up and now everybody wanted to be witness to my incredible luck. As all eyes were on the field, with two outs gone, there was a hush in the skybox. Time-out had been taken by Bill Russell, the shortstop. He leaned down and untied his shoe, took it off, and shook a "pebble" out. This just about caused anarchy amongst my constituents. I was on a prepared roll.

The next couple of innings went by without much action, unless you count the hairdresser the guys found in the next skybox who liked to roll dice. The guys knew all about fun!

In the ninth inning, with a 12-to-2 lead for the Dodgers, an extraordinary thing happened. Tommy Lasorda took out Doug Rau, the starting pitcher, and called in Andy Messersmith. Still-recovering Andy Messersmith. Lasorda had found out they were playing golf (that's a no-no) and wanted to make a point to the other players. Andy didn't have his usual movement on his fastball, the movement was in his head. He groped through two outs with hard-hit balls to the outfield and stared at Steve Yeager for the sign. Time-out was called.

The bet was Red Adams, the pitching coach, was to come to the mound between the second and third outs. It was a 12-to-2 rout, that couldn't happen. 50-to-1. Bets down.

As Andy looked through bloodshot eyes toward the dugout, Lasorda was walking out to the mound just passing the third-base coaching box, with Sutton in pursuit. Seems like Tommy John had directed Lasorda out to the mound, and upon checking his sheet, Sutton saw it was supposed to be Red Adams.

Don grabbed a startled Lasorda by the back pocket and directed him back toward the dugout, as Red Adams was told by Tommy John to get to the mound. "Don't ask, just go to the mound and turn around." Red responded, and he and Lasorda passed each other with an inquiring glance.

Red came to the mound. Andy looked at him and said, "What in the hell are you doing out here?"

"I think it's some kind of a bet Sutton and John are mixed up in," Red said.

"I'm going to *kill* McCord," cried an overworked Messersmith. Red left the mound scratching his balls like a good coach.

The skybox went berserk, vitriolic and vituperative phrases were thrown my way. All of them went unnoticed as Mad Dog and I were adding up our bets.

There were cries of "Fix," and "Setup," as I was collecting bets. Unemployed Lloyd, one of our resident point-setters, told me it was the luckiest day he had ever seen a guy have since Fairway Louie married into "real money" on his fourth try. Unemployed told me he would have to catch me later, he was a little light today to cover his losses.

I looked at Mad Dog, and he looked at me, and we both knew

we couldn't collect on this act of deceit. I told everybody who would listen that all my bets were called off because "I had entered an agreement with some of the Dodgers."

"I knew something was strange when you left early to get prices for a 'tuck and roll' in Tijuana. Everybody knows the best 'tuck and roll' is in Mexicali," lamented Unemployed Lloyd. "I love you, man," he directed at me, after my announcement.

The ball game was over and the dice game was going strong. Just as Mad Dog and I were leaving, we turned and heard the hairdresser say as she was heaving the dice, "Come on, hard five, I'll manicure your mama if you bring it home." She brought it all.

Golf's 100-Proof Legend

There are few men who move other men to stories as the day grows weary. Those few who have lived life with a certain panache and ridiculed every attempt at life to corral that spirit will always live in defiance of a code or encumbrance. He greets the day with a guitar and a Hawaiian shirt and grins at the plaintive night. He is vertically worthless, but touches us all on the horizontal. Johnny Jacobs is a giant fun bag.

This Johnny Jacobs is not the golf teacher from across the pond. This Johnny Jacobs is one of golf's great legends, not so much with his golf clubs, but with humor and a swizzle stick. He is on the Senior Tour now, doing well. He spent 1968 to 1980 on the PGA Tour, driving it long and living it fast. He accumulated $110,000 in that twelve-year period and spent over a million. He lets out the shaft in life.

During the sixties while Johnny was in high school, he would take the summers and go on a field trip to the PGA Tour. His brother, Tommy Jacobs (1965 Ryder Cup member and '66 Masters runner-up), would get him a job caddying for Tony Lema, "Champagne Tony Lema," the stylish shotmaker who had a passion for life. Johnny was well tutored.

Growing up near Los Angeles, J.J., as we call him, was a prodigy. He was big at thirteen years of age, 6′1″, and could tattoo that orb into submission. Drives of more than three hundred yards were commonplace and so were Cole Haan loafers and silk pants. J.J. had style. "The game came to him easily, and he could do it all," recalls his brother. Yet Tommy also says, "John was a happy-go-lucky kid. He liked his fun even then. He was capable of doing all kinds of stuff." He was a quick study.

As we encounter J.J. for the first time, it was in the early sixties while qualifying for the National Junior Championship near Detroit, Michigan. J.J. was to fly into Detroit Airport and be picked up by members of the tournament committee in a big school bus and driven to the YMCA by the golf course, where participants were to be housed. Some of these youngsters were away from home for the first time and the parents would rest easy knowing little Johnny would be safe in this environment. Well, not all of the junior golfers watched *Mister Rogers*.

J.J. exited the aircraft from the only place he knew. First class, of course, and he strode right by the little old ladies waiting to pick up the junior golfers and take them to the bus. J.J. was decked out in Gucci loafers, Lacoste golf shirt, handmade Italian gabardine light summer wool slacks, a Lyle & Scott cashmere sweater wrapped around his neck, and a wad of hundreds in his back right pocket. He immediately went to the Hertz counter and picked up his Lincoln Continental with fake I.D. and Tommy's credit card, which had been given to Johnny "in case of an emergency" by his caring brother. J.J. was given directions to the Hyatt Regency in downtown Detroit, where he checked into a suite and ordered room service for the night. Not bad for a sixteen-year-old.

The next day he drove his Continental to the golf course and asked for valet. "All we got is buses here, sir, you'll have to park it yourself," said the attendant. J.J. pulled out a five and handed it to the guy and said, "Don't get it dirty," and strutted into the clubhouse.

After the practice round, J.J. went back to the Hyatt. Feeling kind of lonely in this big city, he went to the phone books and ordered a couple of escorts to the room, along with some fine French champagne. At sixteen, J.J. knew how to party.

A few days later, word got back to J.J.'s brother, Tommy, that his credit card was over the limit. Tommy quickly canceled the card, and J.J. was without the Hyatt or the Continental for the remainder of the tournament. The YMCA, with eight kids to a room, was not the Hyatt, and the ground transportation was now less than adequate. "Here's Johnny" started at a young age.

To say J.J.'s attention span is short is like saying Anna-Nicole Smith needs a bra. J.J. got his college education from the University of Southern California for four days, before he dropped out! This is where he met his lifelong friend, John. John owned a bar next to the campus and J.J. frequented it during his four-day education. J.J. couldn't remember anybody's name, so he calls everyone "Luke" to this day. Luke taught J.J. everything he knows.

J.J. stayed around and worked out with the golf team, then one day, when coming back from a tournament and a brief stop at a local bar, Luke took over the driver's seat and escorted J.J. back to their apartment. This is usually not a good idea. J.J. remembers lying down in the backseat as Luke pulled into the fast lane of the 415 freeway heading east. George, another golfer, was asleep against the passenger's window and all looked quiet for the ride home.

J.J. was startled by a pounding noise on the car window. He arose from the backseat and peered out the front window, wondering what the sound was. Luke had both hands on the steering wheel, driving like Miss Daisy, foot on the throttle. George was still passed out on the passenger side, drool coming out of the corner of his mouth. Then the resounding thumping sound came again. J.J. tried to refocus his eyes and found out where the sound was coming from. At that moment, Luke rolled down the window of the car with one hand, the other hand trying to maintain control of the car in this desperate situation. He stuck his head out the door, bloodshot eyes still staring at the road straight ahead, asking the officer, "How did you catch me?" J.J. was startled to see the officer standing next to the car while Luke was in full throttle. Luke, as he had pulled out into the fast lane, had shifted the car into neutral, and had been driving with reckless abandon, trying to keep up with all the cars that were passing him in the slower lanes. The officer said Luke had been there for fifteen minutes in a furious attempt to keep up with the traffic. They were all arrested.

Later that year, he ended up in the army and was sent to Vietnam after an escapade with the general's wife. All efforts by J.J.'s friends to "talk some sense into the general" failed. As always, J.J. made the best of it. He scored thousands of dollars on the black market selling broken-down refrigerators with ice stacked in them. He was known as "The Ice King." He also partied with the Vietnamese Army brass and played golf with the premier of the country. Not bad for a Specialist Fourth Class.

After the army, J.J. took to the road in pursuit of his career in professional golf. He needed some money and quickly got a sponsor, a close friend from San Diego named Ray Kwano. Ray was a rancher with enormous land holdings. Ray liked J.J.'s style and friendship. J.J. asked for, and got, $65,000 for the year: a healthy sum in those days to travel the Tour. J.J. felt so obliged to Ray, he asked him if he wanted to accompany him to the British Open that year in Hoylake, England. They got over there early and had a great time playing golf and frequenting the pubs prior to the beginning of the Open.

J.J. had a late start that first day, a 3:30 tee time, and was well awake as he hit the first shot. As he was walking down the second fairway, a voice rang out from the gallery, "J.J., I'm here to watch you play." It was a friend of his from Walnut Creek, California, named Sil Enea. His other sponsor? It seems that J.J. had also reached an agreement with Sil to sponsor him on the Tour for, you guessed it, $65,000. That's $130,000 to play the Tour in 1967. Neither party knew of the other. J.J. had to pay the sponsors back out of each check he earned. Well, if he paid *both* parties a percentage of the check he made, he would have to pay out of *his* pocket to the sponsors. If he made a $100 check, he would owe both sponsors 80 percent of the check, or $80 apiece, $160 for $100 winnings. After only four days in college, he could figure out this was not a good deal! So he would not play in many tournaments and then when the racing season at Del Mar started in the summer, they knew J.J. would be betting on the ponies instead of a three-footer. He had the first year worked out perfectly.

Sil was on one side of the fairway waving at J.J., and Ray was on the other. J.J. had a problem on his hands. For the next couple of hours, J.J. would talk to both and try to keep them from walking on the same side so they wouldn't get together. This was a tough British Open course!

On one particular hole, J.J. was immersed in the complexities of an eighty-yard sand wedge shot to a green hidden down in a hollow. The shot turned out fine, but he lost his two sponsors to the clubhouse that was nearby. Anxiously, he pulled his visor down lower and continued his career.

The bar area was a square configuration, with two bartenders working the pub. Sil sidled up to a seat at one end, and minutes later Ray approached from the other. By Sil's recollection, the conversation went something like this: "Aren't you following the group I've been walking with?" Sil: "Yeah, I believe I've seen you out there. I'm sponsoring one of the players and came over from California to watch him." Ray: "That's funny, I came over here a week ago with the guy I'm sponsoring on the Tour, Johnny Jacobs." Sil: "You can't be sponsoring him, I'm sponsoring the golden boy!"

A short powwow ensued and the numbers were compared. J.J. had played three holes since the evacuation and now, over a hill, strode his two sponsors side by side. They were standing tandem, right by the tee markers so J.J. could not miss them. He hit his tee shot, picked up his ever-present cigarette from the ground, walked over to the pissed-off pair, and said, "I take it you two have met?" Before they could mass an attack, J.J. interrupted, "If you can't afford to sponsor me, you shouldn't have taken up golf in the first place! Let's have a drink in the bar after the round and we'll discuss this pressing matter."

They all met later, and Ray and Sil became the best of friends until Ray's untimely death in an airplane crash some years later. J.J. had once again turned a monetary calamity into a social bonding. He is an extraordinary personality.

J.J. was an institution at La Costa in Carlsbad, California. Tommy Jacobs, his brother, was the director of golf there and J.J. had the run of the place. It was conveniently located only a few miles from his favorite hangout, the racetrack at Del Mar. J.J. made and lost much more money there than he ever won on Tour. He was always hanging around high rollers and always frequented the private boxes, then one day he was gone from La Costa. He'd started to date one of the teamster's girlfriends. The bad news, he was the one running the club. Teamster in, J.J. out, unharmed.

J.J. lived hard on the Tour for those twelve years. Time on the practice tee was cut short due to happy hour and two-for-one drinks at the local watering hole. Del Mar, "where the surf meets the turf," always opened in July, and J.J.'s golf was done for the duration. Ponies and night-marauding were his sidekicks. He was an exotic place waiting to happen.

As long as I've known J.J., he only had one car. It was a 1983 semi-shiny Cadillac with handicap plates. It finally quit, going up the hill to the golf course in Scottsdale, Arizona, where he lives. Sil Enea told me J.J. had wrecked more cars than Earl Scheib could handle, and totaled one motorcycle, in Phuket, Thailand. He is a multinational Super Dave Osborne. He was in worse shape than the motorcycle after the crash in Asia, but he lived to live again. A cat wishes he had this many lives.

Sil Enea had given J.J. a highway patrolman's badge he'd been awarded in Northern California. J.J. was very creative in using the shield to defer the law. During one Tour stop in Houston, Joe Porter, a young barrel-chested, round-mound of sound, inquired of J.J. if he could get a ride to Dallas, Texas, the next Tour stop. J.J. told him he was leaving early the next morning and he had enough room in his rented Ford Galaxy. He would appreciate the company.

Joe showed up promptly at 9 A.M. at the local motel where J.J. was carousing. After he'd repeatedly knocked on the door, a young lady left the room in haste. J.J. announced he would be ready soon. Two hours later, they left for their four-hour ride to Dallas. The first stop was at the 7-Eleven to get some beer for the trip. This was a four–six-pack trip and they needed ice. J.J. got the beer and Joe got the ice. They proceeded to the trunk, where J.J. emptied his shag bag and iced it down with the beer. To the backseat it went. Boy, he's not a virgin at this, Joe thought. Off they went on this boring ride, fully medicated with Bud and Elvis Costello blaring on the radio. Life was good.

J.J. slunk low down in the driver's seat. It was a long night for him and he wanted to get as comfortable as he was dressed. He had on loose-fitting Levi's, Cole Haan loafers with tassels, no socks, and a T-shirt that had the Three Stooges on the back poking each other's eyes out. A two-day-old beard and he'd forgotten to blow-dry his hair. Everybody loves a sharply dressed man.

He always liked to look at the sky while he was driving; it relaxed his golf nerves. The paved road just got in the way of his car. Joe was busy restocking the shag bag and making a neat pile for the empties. He was also in charge of the tunes. The team was in sync.

J.J. was trying to flatten those Texas gullies with raw speed. That Galaxy would really get rumblin' after you had your foot through the firewall for twenty minutes. It was sucking gas and asphalt and it was pegged out.

They came over one deep gully and bottomed out, sparks flying everywhere. Joe's head hit the upholstery on the roof, and J.J. actually sat up for a second, but gravity pushed him back in his recline again. As J.J. looked back, he noticed a patrolman in full pursuit, lights grinning at him through his rearview mirror. J.J. sucked on his cigarette and announced to Joe he had better hide the beer cans or their asses would wind up in a small-town jail. Joe was working hard emptying one suitcase of its contents and refilling it with dead Budweiser cans. Joe should have worked in Ralph's Supermarket, he had the technique.

J.J. pretended he didn't see the cop so Joe could finish his chores. Once done, Joe returned to facing forward, and in a flop sweat wanted to know what was their next move. J.J. said, "The next part could be tricky. My license expired four months ago, but let's see what I can come up with." Joe was feeling like he should know a bail bondsman.

As their car slowed and the patrolman pulled behind him, J.J. got out in a flash and didn't let the startled officer get out of his car. J.J. held his finger on the expiration date of his driver's license and folded over the borrowed patrolman's badge on top of it. "We've been following two suspects in a blue Buick from California. They are suspects in a drug operation centered in Dallas, Texas. We lost a little time with a flat tire about an hour ago and desperately need to catch up before they hit the city." J.J. took a puff of his cigarette and stuck it back in the corner of his mouth. "I haven't got time to sit here and explain myself. If you could oblige us and run interference, we could possibly find 'em."

As the officer looked once more at J.J.'s license, he said, "See if you can stay with us, Mr. Jacobs, it's about an hour to Dallas."

"I'll be like stink on Grandma's underwear to ya," said J.J., with the cigarette waving in the wind as he talked. Lights flashing, the patrol car sped off.

J.J. walked back to the car, slinkered down in his seat, and asked Joe, "Get me one for the road, would ya?" Joe, half-frozen with fright from his impending stay in a Texas jail, stared at J.J. with hollow brown eyes and a painful sweat pouring down his ashen white face, and said, "Are we going to jail?"

"No, we're going to catch some drug dealers from California, and the Texas police are going to escort us to 'em."

"Do you mind if you just let me off here and I'll walk to Dallas?" said a beleaguered Joe Porter.

"If you want, but get me a beer before I let you out. This should be some ride you're going to miss." Joe got J.J. a Bud and decided what the heck, it's a good day to die.

I see a lot of J.J. now. He's a neighbor of mine in Scottsdale. He's slowed down a little. Hell, he should have been dead in the early seventies. I know of no man with a bigger heart or a faster finger on the trigger of life. I cherish the time we spend together and the stories that have made this man bigger than life its ownself.

I toast J.J. with a Pepto-Bismol highball. He's on the Senior Tour now. Good luck, my friend, you'll never be found in the coach section of Delta. You're a first-class kind of guy.

The Globe Open

The city was fertile with expectations of the new Globe Theatre opening at Stratford-upon-Avon: the crowning achievement of life as passion in the year 1598. England was guided in this age of the Renaissance by Queen Elizabeth I. It was an age when men were curious, active, and brave.

William Shakespeare and six other owners had built the Globe Theatre in their trumpeting of the arts. England was alive with purchases of the mind and soul and the festive atmosphere was pervasive. The town of Stratford-upon-Avon was full of mischief as it waited for the opening of the theatre and all the activities that were concurrent with this event.

The town fathers had organized every conceivable adjunct to the festivities, including one that surprised William Shakespeare to "woeful words of plaint." Marcus McCormick, an edacious soul, was an organizer of chivalrous games and employed Sir Peter Dyeabolical, the keeper of the grounds at the Queen's summer mansion, to build a "wooded park with holes." "They must be of such a length as to tire and confuse the performers, and have enough circumstance about the confines to dissuade an errant orb." Sir Peter had a penchant for railroad ties.

The wooded park with holes was in the making for three years prior to the opening of the Globe Theatre, and no one but a handful of peasants who had worked on the project knew of its existence. It was truly a lovely stretch of land born of woods and water, and a peaceful roll of the landscape. It was a place of quiet rest and ready to entertain the performers and plebeian alike.

Marcus McCormick buggied William Shakespeare out into the countryside under the guise of a grouse hunt, but when they pulled up to the grandeur of the old English Cottage, used as the performers' shop, William Shakespeare was taken aback. "What passion has beset this graceful land?" he asked.

Marcus McCormick informed William that he had been working on this quest for the past three years, and wanted to have a performers' goof tournament, called the Globe Open, to coincide with the opening of his theater.

"What in the howling hounds of hell is a goof tournament?" the bard asked.

Marcus explained that two performers parade around the countryside with wooden tools in an effort to persuade a small orb, called a Titleist, into holes discreetly placed into the ground.

"Sounds as if you've invented a game that is so foul of fate it will harvest sinister acts of greed and adultery amongst the men who are consumed by its cries," Shakespeare announced.

"That's a reasonable description of goof," acknowledged Marcus.

Marcus McCormick then told William about the possibilities of making some money out of this performance by selling tickets for the opening of the Globe Theatre, 2,500 seating capacity, and tacking on a couple of pounds for the performance of goof. "The theatergoers wouldst think they're getting a bargain of two performances for the price of one.

"We could sell T-shirts and have the concession of wine and food for the performance of goof and make some more pounds for you and I. I'll only charge you twenty percent of what you take at the gate and get the television rights for five years. What say you, Shakes?"

"I muse at your nurturing of the pound and will not try to hide my mirth at this undertaking. Count me amongst you."

Marcus McCormick had employed two country gentlemen for the past year to work on the nuances of goof and perfect the craft. One gentleman was the Earl of Palmer. The Earl was a tanner and glovemaker, with strong forearms and a flair for life and hitching his pants. He was treated as royalty at Stratford-upon-Avon and was getting in the business of selling Royal Coaches through dealerships located conveniently within the city. He was a riveting character, one who would always go for it, and a good beginning for the stable of Marcus McCormick.

Marcus chose for his other performer a rugged but socially undernourished farm worker. He prowled the wooded fields and slung his E4 swing-weighted ax with a wild arc and with plenty of power. He was of the grip-it-and-rip-it clan of the north. His name was Euripides.

The diversity of these two performers, Marcus mused, would pique the interest of the commoners and make for a rousing introduction into goof, the sport of orb-jousting.

Two orators were to perform the task of bringing the game to the multitudes. Two gentlemen who were renowned conversationalists of the Royal Court. One of the gentlemen had won the National Open of Orators back in 1564 on a sweltering day; his name was Venturus.

The other orator was an upstart in the Royal Court, a man-boy of swaggering confidence, but one who came out of a less than academically accepted university called Houstus. He made up for his shortcomings of intellect with wild bravado and stinging self-assurance. His name was Nantzalot.

It was a great team that Marcus had melded. They would announce from the royal tower that was behind the last wooded hole in the park. It was a perfect place for the spectators to watch and do the royal wave to the Queen Mother. Sometimes a beach ball would appear and the spectators would joust the ball about in a playful manner. These were great times, the Renaissance.

The keeper of the grounds, Dean Bemus of Toursgate, found a beautiful, natural amphitheater for the last wooded holes. The spectators had a great vantage point to view the performers finishing this game of mirth and folly called goof.

We begin our play on the last two wooded holes. The play between the Earl of Palmer and Euripides has been spirited. Let's listen to the orators' comments as they provide the expert analysis.

Act 17, Scene 1

SIR NANTZALOT: Well, Venturus, seems like the Earl of Palmer has hit into the trees again. Can he continue making these marvelous recoveries to keep abreast of young Euripides?

VENTURUS: The Earl of Palmer seems to be finding refuge in the shadow trees. But, for the moment, looks to have grave concern written over his brow.

Let me quote Shakespeare from Arcite, *The Two Noble Kinsmen:* "It's not mad lodging here in the wild wood, cousin?"

Sir Nantzalot, he has got to prod the orb with more precision if he is to seek the hole more efficiently.

SIR NANTZALOT: The Earl of Palmer seems to be in a paroxysm of rage following that shot he failed to get out of the woods. What do you make of this outrage so late in the scuffle?

VENTURUS: "The brain may devise laws for the blood, but a hot temper leaps o'er a cold decree." Portia, *The Merchant of Venice*.

SIR NANTZALOT: Well stated. As the performers approach the precisely cut moss that hides the seventeenth hole, what do you think is going through the mind of young Euripides as he is but a scant one wooded hole down to the Earl of Palmer?

VENTURUS: "Our doubts are traitors, and make us lose the good we oft might win, by fearing to attempt." Lucio, *Measure for Measure*.

SIR NANTZALOT: Venturus, you seem to be in good witness this day!

He has the heart as big as the oxen, and a stomach to match from all the M&M's he has betaken to curb his addiction to haggis and the wine.

VENTURUS: He has taken it upon himself to see Betty of Ford for guidance in this area and we all wish him luck in his quest to rid himself of these demons.

That was a magnificently created prod that Euripides hath made. Can you account for that wonderful conclusion to this wooded hole?

SIR NANTZALOT: "Things done well and with care exempt themselves from fear." King Henry, *Henry VIII*.

VENTURUS: That was a wonderful quote, you seem to be in good form yourself, my tower mate.

SIR NANTZALOT: This is a lovely wooded park where this match has been performed; what do you make of the beauty?

VENTURUS: "As those whose beauties proudly make them cruel; For well thou know'st to my dear doting jewel." *Sonnet CXXXI*.

SIR NANTZALOT: With retorts like those, you're sure to make The Rudy of Gullible's column in the Stratford-upon-Avon's *Today* section. An honor it is, and the theater owners from the land read it with fervor. He can make you or harass your doting ass into Yorkshire county.

Act 18, Scene 1

SIR NANTZALOT: Well, it comes down to who wants the better of the performance and who does not want the bastard's shame.

VENTURUS: I have seen no greater heart than that of the Earl of Palmer. The people have marched with him through the wooded forest with the zest of a fair maiden's love. They troop as one, giving their crusader a lift of heart. It is a loving army that follows this glovemaker.

His fortitude reminds me of a line written by Shakespeare about Venus and Adonis: "The sea hath bounds, but deep desire hath none."

SIR NANTZALOT: Well, Venturus, it's come down to this for the final curtain.

This is the prod that could win the performance for the Earl of Palmer. Hush as we await their fate, oh! A finer shot off the water closet I have never witnessed. It careened off the potty where Queen Elizabeth the First had been temporarily residing and burst into the hole on the moss to win the performance. A staggering defeat for Euripides! A glorious moment for the Earl of Palmer.

SIR NANTZALOT: Venturus, what claims do thee have on that prod?

VENTURUS: " 'Tis a lucky day, boy, and we'll do good deeds on't." Shepherd, *The Winter's Tale*.

SIR NANTZALOT: Let's go down to the wooded park and get the loser's song of lament. We will throw it to our esteemed colleague, Ben of Wrightwood, to do dialogue with Euripides.

BEN OF WRIGHTWOOD: "Grief boundeth where it falls, not with the empty hollowness, but weight." Duchess of Gloucester, *Richard II*.

Is that how your feelings are, Euripides?

EURIPIDES: "Be wise as thou art cruel; do not press my tongue-tied patience with too much disdain; lest sorrow lend me words and words express the manner of my pity-wanting pain." *Sonnet CXL*.

SIR NANTZALOT: Ben of Wrightwood, can you approach the Earl of Palmer for a brief word on his performance?

BEN OF WRIGHTWOOD: I shall. He is now comforting the Queen Mother after her near mishap in the water closet. She seems to be shaken but not stirred.

The Earl of Palmer, might I have a word with you? What sayest you after this glorious day?

THE EARL OF PALMER: "O, such a day! So fought, so followed, and so fairly won." Lord Bardolph, *Henry IV, Part II*.

BEN OF WRIGHTWOOD: Now, let's go back to the tower and Nantzalot and Venturus.

NANTZALOT: A winner was this performance, I'm certain, this inaugural Globe Open. It will add great pleasure to the opening of the Globe and draw due praise for the performance of goof and all that it beckons. For Venturus and myself, we will say good-bye and have it down to our colleague, Ben of Wrightwood, as he talks to the Queen Mother.

BEN OF WRIGHTWOOD: Your Highness, what do you have to say, having witnessed the first performance of goof on this wooded park?

QUEEN MOTHER: Ben of Wrightwood, I would love to pursue this game myself. Do you think I could become worthy of its cause?

BEN OF WRIGHTWOOD: You would make a lovely patron of this game, but I daresay I think your royal boobs might get in the way of your prod!

VENTURUS AND NANTZALOT: Say "Good fortnight," Ben.

BEN OF WRIGHTWOOD: Good fortnight, y'all, and I'll see you at the guillotine!

The Dark Side of the Day

Jonah Jett was a high school tailback from Mill Creek, Oregon, just outside of Portland. A quality boy who was raised in a tight family surrounding, which provided plenty of guidance. His prowess on the gridiron had every scout from Notre Dame to Georgia Tech at his door offering a secure future, but Jonah was always on the golf course putting his considerable athletic skills to work on the game he would not acknowledge he played.

The year was 1969, and if you had an inclination to play golf at the age of eighteen, you dared not let your friends know. Golf was a "geek sport" for those who belonged to the chess club at Mill Creek High School. You had to wear black horn-rimmed glasses and have those pen protectors in your shirt pocket to acknowledge this sport for fat, old men. Whatever your old man did, you despised it with vigor. Jonah's dad loved the game of golf and Jonah was with him as much as possible on the course. Jonah was different than the rest of the boys.

Jonah had a beautiful motion with the golf club. It was a long, high arc that produced plenty of speed to the shots that landed softly on the wet greens of the Northwest. His competitive nature made his jaw set as he battled the local hotshots and learned the game. He shifted his interest in the next few years, much to the dismay of his football coach. In his junior year, he decided to give up his scholarship in football and concentrate on golf at Arizona State.

In the warm climate of Arizona, Jonah played golf by day and studied by night. The last two years went by as fast as a shooting star in the desert sky. He played on the school team the last year and made it as the sixth man. He had all the tools, but lacked competitive experience. With his degree in hand and his college sweetheart, Jill, in tow, he set off for a life on the mini-tours as a professional golfer.

Financial security is not in the equation of mini-tour golf. Basically, players ante up money for the purse and the organizer takes 10 percent to run the event. One golf course is rented during the summer in Florida, when the season is slow, and 180 players lock seven-irons and beat each other silly trying to make expenses and develop their games. It's Darwinism on the back nine and many are ultimately rendered extinct.

In the early years there were a few Don Kings involved in this circus event and the money went elsewhere. South American countries were a haven for the few. Jonah, with financial help from his father, toiled and learned the game well enough to qualify for his Tour card in 1973. Jill and Jonah were married shortly after and set out on Tour in the winter of '74. Money was short, so they spent all they had on a used twenty-seven-foot Fleetwood motor home, put all their belongings on board, and set out for fame and fortune on the PGA Tour. The quarters were cramped, but the future was endless. So was the road.

They arrived at the first stop, which was the L.A. Open, and waited for the Monday qualifying round, which was spread over two golf courses, L.A. North and Rancho Park. They parked their "motor roller," as they called it, in the parking lot of Rancho Park and made this space their home for the week. L.A. North is very private and a driver would be shot on sight if one drove up the entrance. Random shooting, they would call it.

As the news got to Jonah and Jill, they were grilling hamburgers on the butane stove in the parking lot. Only one spot per golf course, 360 players involved altogether. Because this was winter, all the PGA club pros from the north were on vacation and trying to qualify for the early Tour events. Life was not fun at this time of the year for the aspiring young Tour player trying to jump-start his way to stardom. The numbers were against him.

The caddies started to arrive and Jonah had to find a tested Tour caddie he could count on to show him the ropes and lead him through this labyrinth of adversity known as the PGA Tour. The caddies were trying to find a "ride" that could take them to fame and fortune, or at least earn enough money to have their own motel room and not share it with five other derelicts. Life's struggles were simple for the pro looper.

Just before Jonah was going to bed on Sunday night, there was a knock on the door of the motor roller, and a slight black man was inquiring about a job for the next day's qualifying. He told Jonah he had worked for guys like Raymond Floyd and Bert Yancey and needed some young blood to start off the year. He was a nervous sort, as Jonah recognized, and even through the darkness would not look Jonah in the eye, and kept exchanging feet on the three-step ladder leading up to the motor roller. Jonah was tired and asked the slender shadow what his name was.

" 'The Docta' is what they call me," said the high-pitched

voice, "and I'll see you one hour before we tee off right here at the mota home." He was taking charge already. I like that, Jonah thought.

The next day provided his first look at the new caddie. The Docta was half Puerto Rican and half "lower Harlem," as he would say. He was fond of chatter and lacked weight. He had lazy eyes that were surrounded by freckles and short hair covered by a dirty Titleist hat. The Docta was always on call at the ball before Jonah got there and the information was precise. They got along great and Jill liked the way they worked as a team. Jonah shot 70 that day and was down the road to the Bob Hope Desert Classic. It took 65 to get the single spot at Rancho Park. Welcome to qualifying.

There were not a lot of ups and downs the first few months of the 1974 season, just downs. Jonah was playing well, his high score was 71 for the first ten tournaments, but Jonah failed to get into a PGA Tour event. Jill was getting depressed and threatened to go back to Oregon. She had few friends on the Tour and was getting restless with their nomadic life. Jonah and Jill were on the golf course all day and then into their rolling home for the night. The boredom of nonexistence was beginning to shatter their dream.

They decided Jill would return home for a while and live with his parents, and Jonah would stick it out on the Tour. The days were getting longer as Jonah would practice his patience on the course during the day and live in the motor roller at night and call Jill. Most of the conversations ended with tears. She wanted to be with him, but couldn't stand the life on the Tour.

The Docta moved into the motor home with Jonah and they traveled the States together. Jonah's golf game was steady, but he couldn't deal with the nervousness of playing in a tournament. He couldn't handle the fact that if he missed the cut he may not get into another tournament for weeks or months. This anxiety was suffocating him.

They were in New Orleans now, Jonah had not been home in two and a half months. The Docta hadn't been home for ten years. It was a rainout, and caddie and player were discussing how they were going to get it going for the first round of the tournament on Friday. Thursday had been canceled. "How did you ever get the name 'The Docta,' anyhow?" asked Jonah.

"I was a pre-med student in Puerto Rico and wrote phony prescriptions for the other caddies out here before I got caught."

"Wrote phony prescriptions for what?"

"Upper, downers, anything they wanted," said The Docta. "One of the caddies turned me in to the cops after a bad ride and I spent eighteen months in jail. I don't write no mo'."

"Well, if you were going to write me a prescription for my nightmare, what would it be?"

"A beta-blocker, called Inderal, would slow the mo for you."

"Let's try it tomorrow. What do we have to lose?" Jonah queried.

"You could lose your grip on reality, man."

"We have to do something to get this career going. Let's do it in the morning."

They went to a pharmacy in Gretna, down by the tournament site, and got their prescription with no problem. Life, as Jonah knew it, would change forever. The first round was euphoric. There was a new calmness to his demeanor and his game started to click. A seventh-place finish and a new, diluted attitude had emerged.

The phone calls home were less frequent and the family was starting to worry. Jill was pregnant, conceived on her last visit, but the news to Jonah was met with ambivalence. This was not like the man she had married, who months ago would have received this news with waves of enthusiasm. Jonah was medicated, but his golf game was improving.

The new lows on the golf course were met with the want of a surge at night. The motor home was a rolling garbage can. Golf clubs and dirty laundry were everywhere. The stench of two rotting wills permeated throughout. Caddie and player had vanished into this non-reality of lows and highs in search of success on the PGA Tour. Uppers at night to get going were met with downers late at night to get to sleep. Quaaludes and beer washed down the chips and salsa as the fabricated sleep swept the motor home.

Jonah and The Docta pushed on, walking the fairways with a surreal stride. Remarkably, Jonah was able to forge ahead and keep his game together while his life was falling apart. Jill sensed a roller-coaster personality in his behavior, but Jonah convinced her the toll of the Tour was wearing him down. He couldn't write now because he was playing so well. "I'll be home when my game needs a rest," he convinced her. He needed help, but the motor home trained its headlights on the next Tour stop. They were driving into the eye of the hurricane and there were no storm warnings.

A few ounces of "toot" were bought at the last Tour stop from a local and the boys were loaded up after another top-ten finish by Jonah. He had now won well over seventy thousand dollars in the last five weeks on the Tour. They were now into May and on their way to Texas for the Tour swing there. He had not called home in two weeks. Messages were left on his locker room door by Jill and his father, but none was returned. The world outside of golf was turning dirty.

As they drove into Dallas late Tuesday night, they turned onto 35W and started toward downtown. The motor roller was rockin' with R.E.M. on board from the failing speakers that had been amped to death. They drank beer and had done five lines of semi-dirty powder in the last six hundred miles. The Docta was at the wheel, peering through a dirty windshield, looking for a gas station and some "rock." He cleanly persuaded the motor home into the Texaco station and woke up his boss. Eyes married to the back of his head, Jonah awoke and promptly vomited his sickness away. "Man, you can hit those long irons to death, but you can't do dust worth a shit. I'm going to pack this buzzard's belly with fuel and try to score some 'rock.' Stay alive until I get back." The Docta left the motor home and went out into the chilled darkness.

Jonah passed out immediately and was awakened by the sudden shifting of the motor home on the open road. As he peered through sorrowful eyes toward the front of the vehicle, he didn't recognize the figure behind the wheel. One more glimpse told him The Docta was not in and somebody had control of his motor home. "Who in the fuck are you, and where is my partner?" Jonah's voice rose with urgency.

"I ain't Mr. Rogers, motherfucker!" The driver and the .357 Magnum turned at the same time. For a fleeting moment, Jonah saw Jill four months pregnant, then he saw darkness.

The headlines read: FORMER FOOTBALL STAR DIES IN TEXAS SHOOTING. There was no mention of the family that had lost him or the fact that the PGA Tour had been his wasteland for the last few months. The mention of drugs never darkened the space or the Tour's image. The halo of darkness is still preserved.

This story is entirely fiction. Any resemblances to actual people are coincidental.

Father's Day Golf

It wasn't long ago, maybe yesterday, that my dad and I went to the club to enjoy a round of golf on Father's Day. It was Victoria Golf Club, arguably the second-oldest golf course in California. We have enjoyed many days of golf there as I have come off the Tour and needed my mom to do my laundry. Laundry and daybreak are the same for me. I mix whites and darks and it comes out a little hazy.

We settled into the utility vehicle and made our way to the club, my dad armed with the notion that with sixteen strokes he was finally going to whip my ass. There was a strong odor of confidence reeking from the driver's side. We were exchanging barbs as I noticed a roadside stand that was selling hot cider and curiosities. Strange, I had never noticed this stand before and I had traveled this well-worn path for most of my wandering years.

The stand operator was a bearded, semi-hunched-over preboomer who had a tattoo on his arm of an evil-looking spinster who was perched on a concrete coffin that was graffiti-ridden. He told me it was his mother, and she was doing fine. We turned, after a brief conversation, and told him we were off to chase the dimpled ball. Play golf, as we had to explain. He asked if we would like to try some elixir he had been brewing for some years. He had gotten the recipe from an old Crow Indian spiritual healer. "It was a cure for the soul and all that it possessed," he stated. The old coffee-colored glass container had a picture of the stand operator, Dr. Nathan Screaming Tree, on the label. I gave him a five-dollar bill and told him to keep the change. I wasn't about to ask any more questions.

As we proceeded on our short jaunt to the course, my dad decided he needed some spiritual help. He had been married to Mom for forty-seven years; he took a big gulp.

The round started off like most other rounds we have played. I started immediately with the verbal barbs and harassments. But for some reason, this time it did not bother him. His swing and mind had reached a level I have never been witness to before. He played as if he were having an out-of-body experience with Ben Hogan. At the turn, I was three down, gross. My one-under-par score was anemic to his outgoing score of 31, which was his all-time best, by six shots!

I was excited for him, as he handled this metanormal experience as though he does it all the time. Where in the world was this gift coming from? He was now settling into this newfound genius by verbally assaulting my every shot and never letting up with near-perfect shot-making. I was getting a sponge bath on the course from a man who couldn't get within twenty shots of my score. He now had me six shots down with three holes to play. My dad currently stood at eight shots under par!

We usually had a good time drinking beer and running the gas-powered golf cart all over the place. This time he kept refusing my requests to have another cold one and he kept driving that damn thing down the middle of the fairway after his drives, and I noticed the bottle with Dr. Screaming Tree on the label was now half empty. Curious.

I had now given in to the fact that my carcass was his for the first time since I was eleven years old on the golf course. I have never seen him so happy, as he wedged his third shot to gimme range on the closing par-5 for a spectacular 63, nine under par. Not bad for a 16 handicapper.

As we were driving up the path to the clubhouse to tell all his friends that he had put a rented-donkey beating on his Tour-tested son, I noticed that Dr. Screaming Tree's elixir bottle was now empty. "What happened to the bottle?" I asked. He told me after the first gulp it tasted so bad he had poured it out after the third hole. This one did not need Angela Lansbury.

The bar scene was a frenzy of stories and half-truths. He was standing tall in the middle of it all, soaking in the glorious light of victory over his perfect grip son. The moment was his.

As we passed the place where Dr. Screaming Tree's roadside stand had been earlier, my dad nearly turned the color of silica sand, as the area was vacant and no trace of the elixir man was found. Gone as the night wind. We drove home in silence.

As my dad and I had pulled out of the driveway from their house to go to the course for our annual Father's Day massacre at his club, he had told me of a bizarre dream he had had the night before. He noted if dreams come true, he was going to beat the hell out of me today on the course. Right, Dad, and the Colorado Avalanche will win the Stanley Cup, too!

Gary's Subliminal Golf Swing Guide

I would be remiss if I penned a book about the demonic nuisances of this infuriating game and did not include some instruction on the fine art of swinging the club. Many books have been written over the years about the machinations of this diabolical insanity we call golf. To me, most of the books are too long. This is my effort to comfort those who are severely impaired with regard to attention span.

1. Always aim your feet PARALLEL to the target line. The target line is the line made between your golf ball and where you want it to go.
2. You must grip the club in the fingers of both hands, and have the left hand (if you play from the right side) turned to the right, so that there is a cup in your left wrist.
3. You must hit down on EVERYTHING to get the ball in the air. Obviously your driver is on a tee, so try and hit up on that. It will spend more time in the air and you'll have more fun.
4. Try and turn your left shoulder over your right foot on your backswing. That will give you some torque to wallop the ball on the downswing. Don't worry about moving your head.

5. When you're done, you should be facing the target with your belt buckle, and your right knee should be touching your left knee. Hopefully, you'll be standing upright.

There! That's all you need to know about this debilitating exercise. Don't hold me responsible for your failures.

The Golf Swing—Chaos

To sit in the dark doorways of golf's structural template and howl at the inconsistencies of movement is the very nature of chaos. Chaos can be determined, I am told, but not its artistic form and substance. Here I begin the story of knowledge.

The search for bodily transformations in time and space led me astray for most of my fantasy life. Then, as cruel punishment, the dark side of cognition entered my interpersonal world. His name was Phillip McGleno.

I knew nothing about the task at hand, but buoyed by fifteen years of exile in the sport of aerodynamic flight, I listened with great intensity. I was rewarded with an evolutionary transcendence that went beyond my own human development. My movement became controlled and so did the point of impact. The puzzle was unwrapped with dignity and perseverance. I will not stray.

He told me of lines of parallel energies and of energy-free distortion. His journey through the mystical bond of ball and soul became my guide. Tales of out-of-body, ego-transcendent forces that move us into new realms of movement captured my fascination. Gravity was no longer a concern.

After hours of interlude, the mundane subculture of golf invaded my privacy once again. This time, however, it was not articulation, but a higher, more spiritual force which drove me.

I was fascinated by my discipline. I found that my line of communication had been scrambled at the pre-motor set position, and so from there I could not function. A simple box of shoulders, hips, and knees with feet aiming to ten and one o'clock was all the integral development I needed.

I established a fixed foveal field with arms hanging vertical, my left hand in 45-degree dorsey flexion, and the same with the shaft to the ground. I was at ease. I had lowered my moment of inertia and did not succumb to weightless flight.

The clockwise motion was easily understood, because as early primates we evolved with electrical machinery that had been handed down through millions of years by the left side of our brain hemisphere. The mapping was there.

To control the trajectory is everything, the path and club face will determine the curve. Mid-backswing shaft to right elbow is essential for the correct plane; we are in closed-loop neurological movement at this time, and control is ours. Starting our descent, we must establish the balance-writing system in a full Sam Snead squat. We are now in open neurological control and nothing can be stopped. At this point, we have a choice in the matter of trajectory, and I chose to guide my shaft to mid-humerus level. I am still maintaining full-gaze control with my eyes to ensure all balance systems are stabilized. We have contact for .005 seconds. I feel like I've been here for a long time.

The through part of this swing is a combination: torso tilts to control trajectories, and a switch of power from the primary to the secondary side to ensure the efficient transfer of linear thrust to rotary power. We have creatively altered our muscles, organs, cells, and molecular processes in the short span of a golf swing. The metamorphosis has begun.

The mystical blending of structural enhancement and social deformities must now begin. Marcel Mauss published a paper called "Les Techniques du Corps," which proposed a three-level study of human nature. He said in this paper, "We are everywhere faced with physio-psycho-sociological assemblages of series of actions." The alignment of these will lead to metanormal survival. The choice is today, the consequences are told tomorrow.

The dark side of the light is the only door that now lies in front of us. Mr. McGleno is the gatekeeper and he isn't telling anyone. He did say once, "When the odor surrounds you, you will be there." Disciplines that affect the flesh as well as the psyche are there for our interpretation. Mac O'Grady is the interpreter, now we seek the language.

The Weirdest Swings on Tour

When I used to wander up and down PGA Tour practice ranges in the mid-1970s, it was like taking a stroll through the Louvre in Paris. This was the Renaissance period of golf swings. The individuality of the game was in full bloom. There was still enough mutation in the species that full Darwinism had not evolved the golfer into the overanalyzed, Zen-heavy cross-creatures we are bound and gagged by today. When I perused the swings of these late-model gas-guzzlers, the grass somehow seemed greener, the air cleaner.

The Tour today is a production line of ramp-model golf swings. They're very pretty to watch, but also spiritually undernourished. Each motion is replicated with bountiful input from golf swing doctors and cutting-edge technology.

It is convoluted madness. We have physiologists, neurophysiologists, kinesiologists, biomechanical experts, and skycaps telling us how to swing. The gateway to learning is so extremely crowded. It has made learning very hard and produced Stepford golfers. They all look like the little guy on the tops of golf trophies. Want a flying elbow? Go rent one.

So how did this era produce the dipsy-doodle, Gumbyesque

swing antics of Jim Furyk? I can fathom the weird methods of Allen Doyle and Robert Landers, the other walking lab experiments. They're a bit older. But Furyk? How did that wild and wonderful swing take root in this day of retro-techno, Golf Channel–induced perfect swings?

Allen Doyle, at forty-eight the oldest rookie in PGA Tour history, is a three-time Walker Cup player with a mystical short game. Allen is 6′3″ and 210 pounds, a big man with a little swing. He learned it as a youngster by practicing in a room with a very low ceiling. He could make a full swing under a coffee table. Allen sets his hands behind the ball at address. He played hockey in college, and I suspect his slap-shot movement with the right hand carried over into golf.

Robert Landers took up the game at twenty-two, working on his seventy-three-acre farm in Azle, Texas. Bored with herding methane-producing cows, he needed recreational stimulus. Robert's finish is earmarked by a lifting of the upper torso and hands. This is socially motivated; I, too, would want to get my nose as far as possible from a fresh cow chip after giving it a whack.

Jim Furyk has the most unusual swing since Miller Barber. The first and last frame is textbook stuff, but the rest looks like a Tilt-A-Whirl amusement ride gone haywire. You're supposed to keep the shaft on a constant plane, but Jim changes planes more than most flight attendants. I think I need some Dramamine.

Swings in the old days were as distinct as fingerprints. Players pursued a trajectory and path born out of feel and wonder. They beat the ball into submission without provocation from a guiding intellect. There was freedom from restraint. They asked not why, they just looked to the sky. Remember the principals? Miller Barber's swing looked like a guy in a dark room flailing at a Mexican piñata with a short stick. The positions of his arms and shaft on the backswing duplicated a samurai warrior raising his sword to do battle. But Miller's downswing looked like Sam Snead's. God love centrifugal force. Weird but wonderful.

Chi Chi Rodriguez's swing was very distinctive. At least I *think* it was distinctive, because he swung so fast I'm not sure I saw it at all. Chi Chi's swing always looked like he was in a room filled with flies and his flyswatter wasn't big enough. Odd but adorable.

I remember Lee Trevino hitting balls next to Snead one day. It looked like the before-and-after picture of the golf Tour's recruiting poster. Come in looking like Ernest Borgnine and we'll send you home looking like Mel Gibson. But there was a method to Trevino's madness. Lee's swing always looked like he was pulling a heavy load with a skinny horse, but a better ball-striker I have not seen. Bizarre but beautiful.

And, as always, perched high on the throne of the range was the king himself, Arnold Palmer. Arnold swung the club as though he were playing tug-of-war with Zeus. Two mythological giants not willing to give in, and empires at stake. Extraordinary and enduring.

Don't forget Nancy Lopez, an LPGA Hall of Famer whose backswing reminded me of someone trying to push open a garage door. Nancy had some of the best tempo in golf, which was nice because if it were quick she'd need clearance from NASA. Idiosyncratic but repeatable.

There was a younger Raymond Floyd. Lots of hair, Ban-Lon shirt, and the half-glazed stare of a demonic accountant. His eyes were everything. Raymond's swing took on the curvilinear arc of an abandoned amusement-park ride. There were dips and sways in all sorts of places. He created an E ticket ride, and we all know how well it worked—and still does. Eccentric and emotional.

These were players who used empirical knowledge to set their courses. Swing preference was deduced from ball flight. There was no accepted norm, so there was no peer pressure to conform.

What are the forces that cause these strange movements with the golf club to manifest? Are they social, environmental, or just physical aberrations of the absurd?

We should examine the term "motor control" to understand how a swing is born.

I have extracted all of my knowledge base of motor control from the book *The Neural Basis of Motor Control* by Vernon Brooks, Ph.D. It is not a fun read. Mac O'Grady force-fed it to me. Motor control refers to the study of postures and movements and also to the functions of mind and body that govern posture and movement. "Posture" is the static position of any part of the body. "Movement" is the transition from one posture to another.

We are born with only rudimentary motor abilities. We have to learn to stand and to walk, to use our hands, to acquire practical skills, to play golf. Motor learning is concerned with the coordination of joints, and as a matter of detail, the muscles that move and hold them. (I'm starting to get a headache.)

Once a movement has been learned, we use a plan of motor action to carry out that particular task. Motor memory is twofold: how it felt to make the effort and what result was achieved by it. *The swing felt bad, but the shot was a Rembrandt; I'll remember that one.*

Which brings us back to Furyk, Doyle, and Landers. How did they learn a method no sane person could conceive, let alone teach?

The answer is, they learned by extremes. Take the club as far outside on the backswing as possible and then drop the shaft as far to the inside as possible on the downswing and then look down the middle. Bruce Lietzke plays about as frequently as I make cuts, but when he plays he's always right there. Why?

If Bruce had to follow the fourteen stations of the cross on his backswing and then duplicate all the postural transformations of a yoga master on his downswing to make a perfect swing, he would be a mechanic at Jiffy Lube right now. Bruce simply aims as far left as he can with his setup, takes the club as far inside as he can going back, and on the downswing performs an over-the-top move of biblical proportions with an open club face at impact. He last hooked a ball in 1975.

Furyk, Landers, and Doyle possess mutations of the golf swing that have sprung forth from the mire. They do it differently and do it well, refusing to acquiesce to those who say it can't work. I doff my visor and salute their pilgrimage.

Keeping in mind that in golf as in life, it can pay to get weird.

A Clockwork Golf Ball

The light had focused as the new generation of golfers appeared on the surlyn horizon. The mystical weaving of technology and modern physical enhancement was reducing the game to a spectator sport of drives that reduced our longest courses to ridicules of brevity. Equipment that enhanced, or as some say, demolished, the very core of golf's playful soul was crowding our pro shops. Money was no object, as the obsession of length and precise contact was everywhere. The new recreational world was upon us, and the strangulation of golf's primal past had been put to rest.

Mind mechanics which put the golfer into secure zones that lasted for months replaced the archaic venue of brief discovery. The mind mechanics technique had been discovered in a joint grant between the New Age mind consortium at Irvine, California, and Nepalese Western Civilization. A combination of structured enzyme mind-enhancing injections and manipulation of the body's electromagnetic field had made pro athletes swarm in the zone for months at a time. Records are being smashed and games are becoming sterile.

In this New Age, golf had become the forefront of techno-research. Virtual reality golf had blossomed. The game had gotten so easy that scores in the lower sixties were commonplace on the New World golf tours. Half the golf population had a handicap of three or less, and drives of 350 yards were the norm.

The new rage was to play golf with a golf swing of your choice merely by selecting a hologram of any golfer who was in the library of curvilinear arcs. You could find these stations at most golf courses or at any supermall. They were all connected to a mainframe in Ponte Vedra, Florida, where the Federation of Golf was located. There were swings of more than 200,000 golfers who had played the professional circuits for millennia.

Let's say I wanted to swing like Byron Nelson. I punch his number on the menu list of my "holo" room. A hologram appears in this space of Byron Nelson swinging a golf club. I view the motor movement to see if this is the one I wish. If so, I verbally confirm and step "into" the hologram and have my motor system corrected to perform this task, my electromagnetic space altered so muscles are reprogrammed to perform this function. Future medicine is cool.

The obvious techno-glut is everywhere and golf is no longer fun. The courses are obsolete. There is no more space to build longer courses to facilitate the length the golf ball is going. The set of clubs consists usually of five ceramic-ti blend distance clubs averaging 900 cubic inches per club and eight wedges of varying groove depths. The only throwback to our past is one putter, although the average length is fifty-three inches. This length helps to offset focal dystonia that occurs as the golfer ages.

We lost the age of discovery and wonder when we used to sling our carry bags on our shoulders and traverse the course searching for clues to flight and control. As a society, we have become immersed in a technological stupor. The feeling of flow has deserted our soul on the golf course.

There is a buzz around the station ranges, that is the new name for driving ranges. You could go to an individual station and have private computer and medical access for your mind exercises as you hit balls into your virtual reality golf station. There are a number of professionals who were not using all the techno resources, and they were playing brilliant golf with less "restraints." There is a flow to their game and a bounce in their step. What is happening?

After a few inquiries, I found that they were going to a former British freedom fighter who had lost the sight in his right eye in wartime engagement. Their excellent play and the fact that this gentleman was producing highly non-techno-absorbing golfers was all I needed to make a call and satisfy my curiosity.

His name was Doc Nightingale and he presided over a nine-hole course called "The Devil's Flashlight" in an old military base in the state of Southern California. These bases are becoming a haven for recreational facilities, since military presence had subsided around the globe due to the influx of retro-aggression drugs that permeated the world's watering system. The world had become silent of turmoil.

Doc was a small man with a hungry frame and a blissful smile etched on his face. We started our golf session a little before sunset. A curious time, I thought.

He asked me what I thought of the golf swing and what it takes to make a living on the New World Tour. I dazzled him with tales of mechanical flight and the arduous preparation of the mind to absorb the social and environmental hazards that floated in time. He seemed to listen, but not to hear.

As the sun set, he was obviously bored with our conversation and we proceeded to the first tee of The Devil's Flashlight with carry bags slung over our shoulders, as he requested. I had no idea what was going on.

"The lesson will be conducted by you," Doc said. This also struck me as strange. "We're going to play nine holes for the cost of the lesson. You win and you don't owe me a thing."

"Why don't you go first," Doc said, with that permanent smile. I could not believe that we were going to play nine holes at night. What could I possibly learn from this nocturnal séance? Did I have enough golf balls for this version of blindman's buff?

There was no possible way this slight, unimpressive man could beat me day or night. I played the New World Tour and have been tested by the best the world has offered. I took exception to his offer.

I glared out into the darkness and asked Doc where in the black void was the fairway. He told me to aim at 11:00 and fade it to 2:00. What kind of directions were these? In my mechanical thesis of the golf swing I have never heard of this target location exercise. I use a digital watch and don't remember the Old World configuration. We spent the next five minutes going over the location of hands on the clock.

As I addressed the ball, it was barely visible through the darkness. I was alone in my thoughts and could not focus on the ball and my cause. This presented a strange anomaly for my didactic observations on golf. Without the ball, I was left to wonder about feel and flight. The mechanical template was lost to lack of sight. Doc had told me to fade the ball, starting it out toward 11:00 and bending it toward 2:00. I didn't know how to hit the shot without going through my five pre-motor directional links to fade the ball. I was lost without visual confirmation.

I stepped back and tried to visualize the flight. I approached the ball and addressed the blurry outline of the golf ball. I knew I had to keep my head steady so I wouldn't get air instead of ball. I kept my body still and turned away and set the club head on a path on the downswing, outside a little to curve it left to right.

For the first time ever in my career, I felt the golf swing. The shape of my swing indicated I faded the ball, but as I looked up I saw nothing. I had to immediately reverse back to the feel of the swing to tell me where it flew. A little on the heel and maybe short of my target, I felt. My God, I had a feeling when I hit the ball. It was a primal flashback!

Doc got up and took a short, concentrated swing that had precision written all over the golf ball. He immediately picked up the tee and acknowledged it was right-center about 327 yards out. That was a precise feel!

We wandered down the fairway and I stumbled across the ball, in the darkness, a little short of where I'd guessed it. You could see only an area of about the size of a coffee table in the dark. This was a tough game! But at least it was found on the right side of the fairway, as I had speculated. Doc informed me the green was long and narrow with bunkers alongside the right hand. The hole was cut back right and would need another fade to get it close. He said I was 167 yards away and to feel the rest.

As I approached the ball to fade it with my medium-depth grooved wedge from 167 yards, my first inclination was to hit *down* on the ball because I was basically blind and needed to feel the ground for security. No clipping the ball off the ground, just hit down at it. The feel of the ball on the club was different in the darkness. There are shadows touching my skin. A flurry of feelings.

The club and the ground kissed simultaneously. The swing felt left to right and solid. "That sounded like a good one," Doc said. I hoped his instincts were good, the darkness was pervasive. My ball ended up in the bunker to the right, level with the hole. Doc was fifteen feet short, dead at the hole. I was starting to believe he had infrared eyes.

I nudged the ball with the leading edge of the sand wedge just to find its location and then backed the club off the ball about four inches. I must swing slow and enter the sand well behind the ball, I thought, so I don't blade the ball way over the green and into the eternal void. Strange, I never thought of that before. And another thing, I have had no mechanical thought on any shot. The blackness was starting to lift.

The sand felt firm as the bounce of the club planed through the sand. I felt no ball on the club, just the explosion of the sand toward the hole. The ball rolled past the hole by four feet and Doc told me the putt was straight. The hole was barely visible. Doc tended the pin and clanked the bottom of the cup and "follow the sweet nectar of the hole" as he proclaimed. No thoughts of mechanics in the putting stroke. "Just follow the sound, stay smooth, and listen to the flush of the ball into the plastic hole. Let your instincts guide your hands toward the goal and free your soul." I was beginning to see with no eyes.

The length of time for a four-footer was exhausting, but the ball found the sound and clanked into the hole. That was the first time I had ever had thoughts of the hole and the anticipation of the ball going into the cup. My thoughts had always been mechanically oriented. Strange, new, simple thoughts.

To find the right clubs to hit, you had to hold them toward the dimly lit moon and guess which loft to use, much like the ancient warriors lifted their swords to the sky just before battle. You had to trudge lightly and feel the ground, conversely the days were lost in rapid steps over the landscape, bemoaning the cynical firestorm of golf. I was energized by the blindness.

The battle continued and I eventually lost the match over the course of nine holes. I had miscalculated on two tee shots and never found the ball. Doc had won and I paid for the lesson.

I never saw Doc again, but the nocturnal teaching stayed with me long after I finished my tenure on the New World Senior Tour at the age of ninety-three. I played with feel and detachment from technological stimuli. I let the game consume me. That quasi-mystical state guided me through endless walks on the course, rich in sensory experiences, free of ego-identification and foolish concerns of ordinary mental prisons. I was free to react, it was the greatest lesson ever and one that set me straight in the trance of golf.

I now know why the wolves howl in the dark of night when everything is spiritual. They're free.

If It's Only a Game . . .

If it's only a game, why does it make me cry?

Listen in, the youth of innocence is about to begin
The lost inferno of reasons why
is settling in with the morning sky
Within the green and blue of another hue

The spirit of the game is lost on the range
I allowed myself to struggle alone
The answers will never be known
The ball was agonizing in the sky, listen to their cry

The process was painful
I was at an age I could not bleed
Desire was ravaging my soul to succeed
The dust and the dirt
The soil of my toil

The Tour came quick, I barely remember the process
The splendor of it all, I was caught up in the ball
It was more social than seed
God, what you must give up to succeed

The first flurry of recognition was lost in wonder
The preparation for flight had no detail
Do I wag the dog or the tail?
It makes me cry, me and my soul of the lost blunder

My wife cried for normalcy and touch
I had no safety net for the fall
At this point I had not much at all
She wept for her dream and we passed in the night
If it's only a game why does it make me cry

The Tour changed my life, it possessed all I wanted
No map to camouflage my anxieties
The dream was dead and I was dying
Here, listen to me mourn filled with scorn

The conviction of failure is hard to swallow
I spend many a night thinking about tomorrow
It can't bring any more dismal hate
I await the passage, will it come too late

It's hard to let go, with all the work and labor
The glitter and laughter, is that all that matters
My wife and child grew up with no father
This life is no good, that is all that should matter

As I get along and things start to change
The glory of the past, was it left on the range
I'm doing well now, life can't be any better
How nice it is to hear, you've done well for yourself, my father

Gary McCord

It's a question of how much to give up
That fantasy that questions your soul
I've given up a lot, and ended up with more
So give yourself a chance, and even the score

So why do I cry if it's only a game
Stick around long enough the answer is never the same
Trust your instincts and have great love
It will only come to push and shove